Thinking Beyond the Test

To Paul, with many thanks for all his work on behalf of educating students to think.

Frank Fair

Thinking Beyond the Test

Strategies for Re-Introducing Higher-Level Thinking Skills

Paul A. Wagner, Daphne Johnson,
Frank Fair, and Daniel Fasko Jr.

ROWMAN & LITTLEFIELD
Lanham • Boulder • New York • London

Published by Rowman & Littlefield
A wholly owned subsidiary of The Rowman & Littlefield Publishing Group, Inc.
4501 Forbes Boulevard, Suite 200, Lanham, Maryland 20706
www.rowman.com

Unit A, Whitacre Mews, 26-34 Stannary Street, London SE11 4AB

Copyright © 2017 by Paul A. Wagner, Daphne Johnson, Frank Fair, and Daniel Fasko Jr.

All rights reserved. No part of this book may be reproduced in any form or by any electronic or mechanical means, including information storage and retrieval systems, without written permission from the publisher, except by a reviewer who may quote passages in a review.

British Library Cataloguing in Publication Information Available

Library of Congress Cataloging-in-Publication Data

Names: Wagner, Paul A., 1947- author. | Johnson, Daphne, author. | Fair, Frank, author. | Fasko, Daniel, author.
Title: Thinking beyond the test : strategies for re-introducing higher-level thinking skills / Paul A. Wagner, Daphne Johnson, Frank Fair, and Daniel Fasko Jr.
Description: Lanham, Maryland : Rowman & Littlefield, a wholly owned subsidiary of The Rowman & Littlefield Publishing Group, Inc., [2016] | Includes bibliographical references.
Identifiers: LCCN 2016031863 (print) | LCCN 2016047787 (ebook) | ISBN 9781475823202 (cloth : alk. paper) | ISBN 9781475823219 (pbk. : alk. paper) | ISBN 9781475823226 (Electronic)
Subjects: LCSH: Thought and thinking—Study and teaching (Elementary) | Thought and thinking—Study and teaching (Secondary)
Classification: LCC LB1590.3 .W34 2016 (print) | LCC LB1590.3 (ebook) | DDC 370.15/2—dc23
LC record available at https://lccn.loc.gov/2016031863

∞™ The paper used in this publication meets the minimum requirements of American National Standard for Information Sciences—Permanence of Paper for Printed Library Materials, ANSI/NISO Z39.48-1992.

Printed in the United States of America

This book is dedicated to several important people in our lives:
To Jeanene Wagner, who generously shares her life both with me and my obsession for philosophy and its applications.
Paul Wagner

To Tucker Eberling and McNeil Earhart-Johnson, who bring The Great Conversation of Humankind to life in so many ways.
Daphne D. Johnson

To Ken Fair and Joanna Fair,
Two good thinkers who make their Dad very happy.
Frank Fair

To Malcolm Daniel McMillan, whose future guides my efforts to facilitate a better thinking and caring world.
Daniel Fasko Jr.

Contents

Acknowledgments ix

Introduction xi

PART I: BACKGROUND FOR THE SCRIPTS   1

1   Critical Thinking and the Schools   3

2   Philosophical Inquiry and the Great Conversation: Bringing the Classroom Home to the Philosophical Crossroads   13

3   Psychological Research and Theories on Thinking   27

4   Establishing a Community of Inquiry in the Classroom   41

PART II: SCRIPTS AND SCRIPTING   51

    Tips for Using the Scripts Successfully   53

5   Elementary Scripts   55

6   Building Your Own Scripts   77

Resources for Further Information: An Annotated List   87

References   93

Author Index   101

Subject Index   103

About the Authors   107

Acknowledgments

With four authors, our acknowledgments begin rightly enough by the debt we each owe to one another in writing this volume. Beyond that obvious indebtedness, each of us have those who have mentored us individually, colleagues and scholars whose work each of us have dedicated ourselves to reading; thus, to make any comprehensive list of acknowledgments would be too lengthy and yet still be far from exhaustive. Consequently, each of us can mention only a few of those who have helped form our professional notions. Any and all the misnomers that remain in this book are ours and the four of us share those alone. Without going into the categories of our individual indebtedness, our truncated lists cover the gamut of our professional experiences.

Paul Wagner is indebted first and foremost to three individuals: Matt Lipman, Israel Scheffler, and Chris Lucas. In addition, his encounters with the following have been invaluable: Lawrence Kohlberg, Pat Suppes, Fred Ellett, Ken Strike, John McPeck, Nel Noddings, and Bill Bondeson. Finally, Nicole Wagner-Wallace, who—at the tender age of five—was his first philosophy student. Together Dad and Nicole shared a life of long distance running and philosophizing. Later in the mid-seventies the sixth-grade students at the University of Missouri Laboratory School became his second set of philosophy students.

Daphne D. Johnson wishes to thank David Henderson, Eren Johnson, Sam Sullivan, and John Huber. The opportunity to work with Paul Wagner and Elizabeth Thomlison helped him enter the Great Conversation. Thanks also go to Ashley Earhart, Tucker Eberling, McNeil Earhart-Johnson, and his parents, McNeil and Sara Johnson, for their constant love and support.

Frank Fair is deeply grateful to his wife, Janet, for her love and support and for her wise counsel based on her years as a public school teacher. Frank also feels a great debt of gratitude to the other members of the Sam Houston State University Philosophy for Children (P4C) Interest Group: Daphne Johnson, Debra Price, Lory Haas, Carol Gardosik, and especially the one who started it all, Olena Leipnik. Finally, Frank would like to acknowledge the inspiration of Paul Cleghorn and Steve Trickey, the two people who were the moving force behind the P4C study in Scotland that they were able to successfully replicate in Texas, and to acknowledge that the replication would not have occurred without the support of the Powell Foundation of Houston.

Daniel Fasko Jr. first and foremost thanks his wife, Sharla, for her continued patience and support with his writing endeavors. He is also thankful for the feedback he received from his coauthors, which has undoubtedly enhanced his contribution to this book.

All of us would also like to thank Carlie Wall and Thomas Koerner of Rowman & Littlefield Publishers for their encouragement and assistance with this book.

Introduction

Arabic students were taught two millennia ago to entertain mathematical puzzles about the movements of the heavens. Jewish children have long been taught to consider puzzles in the Torah and in the rabbinical commentary evolving over the centuries to address these puzzles. The Pythagoreans were enamored with the idea that numbers were the language of a Creator and the key to understanding the universe. Socrates provoked the citizens of Athens to look past the obvious and question more deeply what might be afoot in any ordinary human judgment.

The Nobel Prize–winning economist Amartya Sen pointed out that there were seeds of democratic thinking in Indian writings of over two millennia ago. And it is clear that the Chinese thinkers like Confucius to Lao Tzu pondered paradoxes of all sorts. In short, from around the world, cultures were led to various levels of success because they had within them thinkers who raised questions unsuspected by the masses and developed conceptual tools to probe more deeply into matters than most other people ever imagined.

All these thinkers were engaged in some aspect of philosophy, namely reflective deliberation and critico-creative thinking. Philosophy continues as a catalyst to serious and productive thinking even today. The Ph.D. is a doctor of *philosophy* degree. This was meant to indicate that the holder of the degree was qualified to determine what should count as a legitimate claim to know within a given discipline. In contrast, a master's degree traditionally meant that the holder of the degree has mastered much of what is currently known in a field, its technical resources, and how to find one's way about within the published work of the field.

Again, to illustrate the contrast, the Ph.D. meant that the holder of the degree has gone beyond mastery and understands the principles of research so well that he or she can competently inquire about the nature of knowledge claims within the field. This is to say that such a competent person is prepared to effectively ask "How do we know what we claim to know?" and to offer insights into how such claims can be more thoroughly justified. The holder of the Ph.D. is *not* the only one who can effectively pursue such questions, *but* the Ph.D. is expected to be one who has formally established her authority in pursuing such inquiries.

The wonder, analysis, and provocation toward novel insights are neither products of history alone nor the sole achievements of those holding an advanced research degree. However, those that advance understanding within a field are people who are demonstrably comfortable with doubt and who are enthusiastic about removing unnecessary doubt by pushing forever better answers to questions such as "How do we know what we think we know?" In short, those who advance civilization in its knowledge domains and sociopolitical domains are good thinkers.

As will be explained later in this book, we think that evolution made humans natural learners from birth. We think that there are skills students acquire throughout their schooling that gives focus and amplification to their reflective and deliberate thinking, in short, their "mindware."

In addition to advancing the mindware of students, it is important to develop those dispositions necessary for seeking and sharing truth with others. Teaching the skills can begin in the elementary schools and so can fostering student acquisition of the relevant dispositions. There are programs that develop critical thinking in children, and among the most successful are those inspired by the "Philosophy for Children movement."

Appreciation for the importance and effectiveness of such quests in human educational development is as alive today as it has ever been throughout history. When Robert Coles traveled throughout Africa, India, China, and the United States, he found children, five to nine years old, universally were inclined to ponder how people should treat one another. Coles also found that children naturally ponder whether or not there is a hereafter and an initial creator or act of creation. Gerd Gigerenzer has demonstrated that children as young as five or six are interested in risk analysis and are naturally disposed to doing it a bit better with each try.

In short, while evolution prepared human beings for philosophical reflection and analysis, it is important for educators to build on that natural impulse. Evolution prepared people to engage in ever more reflective and deliberative mental activity. However, "pop" culture, the media, schooling, many current education practices, and other influences militate against the exercise of deliberative and reflective thinking. This is alarming since such a result decreases a person's chance for survival, success, and a sense of personal autonomy. Communities want something much better for their children and for the well-being of the communities themselves.

In the United States many tools for developing critical thinking are available even if too seldom used. Unfortunately, there are many more heavy-handed, though well-meaning, government interventions that have impeded the development of such skills in many of the nation's elementary and secondary students today. No Child Left Behind (NCLB) and standardized state curriculums geared to high-stakes multiple choice testing are well-meaning interventions that have led curriculum design and teaching strategies away from developing thoughtful and autonomous young adults.

In the pages that follow, there will be no one-size-fits-all solution to the sorts of concerns identified immediately above. What this book offers instead is a set of strategies for reintroducing higher-level thinking skills into the classroom within the environment that most teachers now labor in. In addition, this book reinforces the idea that there are dispositions that must be developed for students to enter fully into the world of the Great Conversation of Humankind.

Part I of the book describes the theory and science behind the best critical thinking practices. Chapter 1 presents a survey of critical thinking and the schools, and chapter 2 introduces the umbrella notion of "the Great Conversation of Humankind." Chapter 3 is devoted to a survey of research highlighting what can be achieved through focused instruction in higher-level thinking skills, while chapter 4 describes in greater detail the formation of a community of inquiry.

However, the book is first and foremost a toolbox of strategies and scripts that a teacher can learn to use at those teachable moments that still arise in classrooms. Consequently, part II presents sets of scripts that can be used at various grade levels. Chapter 6 encourages the reader to write his or her own scripts. The scripts and other exercises are not intended as a stand-alone curriculum or as an alternative to the sort of standardized curriculums found currently throughout the public schools. Rather the materials herein are available for fitting into a wide variety of curriculums and teaching strategies at a moment's notice.

While the scripts develop higher-level thinking in their own right, they also enrich the standard curriculum in any context in which the instructor recognizes an opportunity to induce students into thinking deeply about matters learned in the standard test—recognition fashion. The scripts also allow teachers to bridge the current "knowledge silo" approach to curricular content and allow students to get a feel for how subject matters overlap and cross contrived intellectual borders.

The training required to teach teachers how to use these materials is minimal and can easily be included in many teacher-training courses. The teacher just needs to know how to use the scripts, and, more importantly, the book can ideally serve every practicing teacher by being kept on the desk in easy reach for that vitally important "teachable moment." Indeed, some parents may even find it useful in that fashion.

The authors involved represent over 100 years of experience from several disciplines in bringing students into the dialogue that is described as the Great Conversation of Humankind. Each chapter has been written collaboratively to bring together all the scholarship and experience of the authors in order to reveal to readers the potential for critical thinking instruction in public school education.

Part I
BACKGROUND FOR THE SCRIPTS

Chapter 1

Critical Thinking and the Schools

Whether you are a student in a classroom, a worker in an office, or a soldier in a battlefield, the ability to think quickly and critically is vital. Identifying all the options, evaluating their pros and cons, and choosing the best option can determine the level of success.

Employers, counselors, parents, and leaders in all situations know the importance of critical thinking in their fields (Kettler, 2014). Indeed, a recent national survey of business and nonprofit leaders in the United States revealed that "more than 75 percent of those surveyed said they want education to focus more on critical thinking, complex problem solving, and written and oral communication" (Hart Research Associates, 2013, p. 12).

Employers are frustrated by the lack of critical thinking abilities possessed by many of their young hires (Bloch & Spataro, 2014; Taylor, 2009). Meanwhile, generations of corporate officers continue the same operating protocols and practices because "it has always been done that way" despite evidence that other protocols and practices might be more effective. Corporate officers manage too often with a focus on past successes rather than thinking toward future success under evolving conditions (Calgren, 2013; Frisbee & Reynolds, 2014).

To compete in the international economy more effectively things must change, and it will take better thinkers to make changes happen. Individuals, corporations, and communities of all sorts need to be more ready to adapt to shifting problem frames.

However, there is a large gap between acknowledging the importance of critical thinking skills and developing them (Weissberg, 2013). The psychologist Jean Piaget (2011) appreciated this distinction long ago when he distinguished between assimilating what is known and the challenge of accommodating one's cognitive architecture to shifting frames of reference.

Learning to *accommodate* changing frames of reference is what higher-level thinking is all about.

In contrast, the process of *assimilation* is just learning facts, protocols, and scenarios as other people already generally accept them (Gigerenzer, 2008). Neuroscience has even shown that there are separate neural pathways employed in higher-level thinking, especially involving the prefrontal cortex (Sternberg, 2016).

The Alliance for Excellent Education (AEE, 2011) notes that critical thinking skills are necessary for every individual to function as effective and responsible global citizens. Forty-eight of the fifty states have adopted the new Common Core Educational Standards. Ostensibly, these include efforts to increase critical thinking among elementary, middle, and high school students (Murphy, Rowe, Ramani, & Silverman, 2014). Yeh (2002) believes that contemporary assessment practices requiring more evidence of critical thinking are evolving. If this turns out to be true, then there must be greater integration of critical skills into daily classroom content.

Teacher educators will be expected to integrate more critical thinking strategies into teacher preparation programs. Teacher candidates will need to learn, practice, implement, and modify effective strategies to challenge their own students' thinking. For this to happen, educator preparation programs must embrace the current research base concerning deliberative and critical thinking and contribute to this body of knowledge.

More importantly, teacher education programs, through this instruction, must convince teacher candidates that critical thinking is important for all students and not just high achievers (Torff, 2005). Unfortunately, many programs that encourage critical thinking are offered exclusively to the gifted and talented students. It is important to note, however, that all students can benefit from the opportunity to engage in critical thinking discussions, activities, lessons, etc. To encourage all students to become more effective thinkers, their critical thinking skills must be developed both across the curriculum and in their daily lives (McCollister & Sayler, 2010).

While the need for better critical thinking skills is well established, Jeffery Sachs, a Columbia University economics professor and consultant to the United Nations Development Council, laments that there are powerful forces whose best interest is in keeping the public from developing critical thinking skills. He explains that the forces of Madison Avenue and politicians generally find it in their best interest to keep people vulnerable to influence by nothing more than a thirty-second commercial. People who become more investigative and look for deeper understanding may not buy products and candidates so readily.

In addition, the costs of informing a more discriminating public could become substantial for those in the business of shaping mass behavior. These forces may avow support for the so-called critical thinking, but what they support in its stead are protocols and practices that in the end do little more than secure student commitment to consumerism and favored political ideologies (Sachs, 2011; see esp. chap. 3). These faux approaches to critical thinking must be avoided in order to meet the goals of the AEE and other professional organizations of educators for the enhancement of students' critical thinking.

If critical thinking is further elevated in the curriculum as some expect and many hope, there must be greater attention to developing both teacher and student skills at asking exact and penetrating questions (Paul & Elder, 2011) and at properly framing problem sets (Kuhn, 2015). Undisciplined speculation and an inability to construct revealing problem sets make the development of critical thinking impossible from the very outset. The materials offered in the later chapters of this book will help teachers and students develop more exacting questions and more effectively learn skills of framing problem sets.

Framing problem sets involves both immediate astute observation and familiarity with reliable primary and secondary research sources. In short, students must learn skills for evaluating knowledge claims. Checklists of valuable resources have been developed by some researchers (McCollister & Sayler, 2010), and in this book, we show how the pursuit of "How do you know?" questions reveals the credibility of such sources when competing claims are at issue. An opportunity to practice these skills in the classroom encourages critical thinking, and it prepares students for more difficult decisions later in life (McCollister & Sayler, 2010).

MAKING CLASSROOM CONVERSATIONS BETTER LEADING TO "THE GREAT CONVERSATION"

Classroom "conversations" can sometimes reduce to homilies and at other times become time-wasting purposeless distractions (Kuhn, 2015). In fact, when discussions lack focus, they can cause a decline in critical thinking. To avoid this decline, there must be an authenticity in the truth-seeking orientation of all who participate in a given discussion. Effective discussions aim at developing higher-level thinking skills and participant acquisition of supporting dispositions such as truth-seeking idealism balanced by responsible skepticism.

This shared truth-seeking ideal forces students to engage directly with one another, to listen, consider, argue, and respond to their peers. The reader should note that "research has shown, this meta-level reflection becomes more extended and interactive, as the effort is made to reconcile opposing positions . . . engage in talk about their thinking" (Kuhn, 2015; p. 49).

The managed balance between truth seeking and skepticism results in students' thinking, questioning, arguing, and responding to their own thinking, as well as the thinking of others with respect and collaborative deference. There will be much to say about this interactive dialogic in every chapter of this book. Presenting students with open-ended problems and teaching them proper etiquette for discursive engagement are necessary for creating the community of inquirers that animates the Great Conversation of Humankind.

DELIBERATIVE AND REFLECTIVE THINKING

"Deliberative thinking" is thinking that is meticulously deliberate. Deliberative thinking avoids a rush to judgment. Deliberative thinking takes time to ponder any and all available pieces of evidence in order to get things right.

"Reflective thinking" is a closely associated concept and is one that is self-aware. Psychologist and Nobel laureate Daniel Kahneman (2011) refers to reflective thinking as "slow thinking" that evaluates the strengths and weaknesses of evidence deployed to support a belief. When people are reflective in their thinking, they are keenly aware of the many ways knee-jerk assessments of others' views or one's own observations can lead thinkers astray.

In recent years, many scientists and philosophers have sought to flesh out the details of deliberative and reflective thinking. From neuroscientists discovering the significantly potent role of the prefrontal cortex in higher-level thinking to the bifurcation of thinking processes between higher and lower levels explored by cognitive scientists, we have refined the study of higher-level thinking (Kahneman, 2011; Thaler, 2015).

But because this is intended in the end to be a practitioner's book, the goal is to move as quickly as possible into the use of scripted protocols for developing higher-level thinking. Before we can do that, however, it is worth drawing the reader's attention to the science, experience, and normative philosophies, which form a basis for the instructional tactics, recommended in the use of scripts. The more exacting approach we offer in scripted discussions in this book can be seen to fulfill the ambitions of higher-level thinking as recommended in the theoretical taxonomies by Bloom (1956) and Sternberg (1994).

Thinking Critically

According to Brookfield (as cited in Fasko, 2003, p. 144), "When people think critically they seek out . . . assumptions for the evidence and experiences that inform them." The point here is that critical thinking begins as gullibility ends. For example, notice as children mature they begin asking "why" for so many of the dictates adults had previously directed toward them. At first they engage in pestering adults with "why" questions for a variety of psychological reasons.

But as children mature they develop "crap detectors." They become more deliberate in what they ask, and they reflect on what they are told. If what they are told does not seem to hold up well in their reflections, then their maturing minds will initiate further questions. If there is a mismatch between what they are now told and their background knowledge, they are disturbed.

As young minds mature (and not just age) they are less willing to leave disturbing mismatches to rest alongside one another in their assimilated repositories of alleged facts. Echoing the psychologist Leon Festinger's (1957) ideas about cognitive dissonance, Brookfield (2003, p. 145) says these of maturing minds, "Critical thinking usually begins with an event that points out a discrepancy between assumptions and perspectives that explain the world satisfactorily and what happens in real life."

Cognitive dissonance exists when it becomes evident to deliberate and reflective thinkers that two facts or two positions cannot comfortably remain aligned side by side. In the maturing mind of a truth-seeking critical thinker, there is a demand to seek resolution of the apparent dissonance. In critical thinking this resolution need not be addressed in binary terms of truth or falsehood, but instead may be resolved finding grounds for giving a greater tentative edge to one position over another.

As Diane Halpern (1998, p. 450) states, "Critical thinking refers to the use of those cognitive skills or strategies that increase the probability of a desirable outcome." Dissonance is what often alerts students to seek a more plausible explanation as the most desirable of outcomes. Halpern's point is that, while students should be truth seekers, they need to recognize that securing optimal plausibility in each case is a matter of drawing conclusions with the best chance of success. In order to optimize plausibility and remove dissonance, students must learn how to gather relevant evidence and evaluate its credibility.

Relevance means that the evidence gathered applies to the situation at hand. Evaluating the credibility of the evidence goes further by assessing its probative force. And there is more that students must learn to be truly critical thinkers. Students must also learn to carefully define terms and to avoid fallacious lines of reasoning. Students must learn that the more clearly terms are defined, the more effectively they can be used as tokens of public intellectual commerce. In short, the use of clear and precise terms increases the likelihood of securing shared understanding.

But even with carefully defined terms in hand, reasoning can still go afoul because of fallacious reasoning. Fallacious forms of reasoning are often common patterns of aggregating thought that seem persuasive—but that are systematically misleading! The statement "everyone says so, so it must be true!" is a common example of fallacious reasoning. Truth is not a matter of calling for a vote. Whether people vote the earth is flat or spherical, the shape of the earth is unaffected. The world and accurate facts that describe it are what they are, and nothing else.

The "everyone says so" fallacy is common among students and many adults alike (the so-called *ad populum* fallacy in informal logic textbooks). The "everyone says so" fallacy systematically misleads thinkers to give too much credence to a weakly relevant observation. The skill to identify fallacies such as "everyone says so" or confusing correlation with causation, or relying on the testimony of illegitimate "authority" increases the thinker's chances of avoiding error and unnecessary cognitive distress.

In addition to skills, critical thinkers must also acquire dispositions supportive of those skills. Those dispositions involve not only truth seeking as mentioned above but also acquiring a laser-like focus on what a person hopes to achieve when settling into a higher-level thinking challenge (Flynn, 2016). Putting skills and dispositions together one might conclude, as Robert Ennis (2011a, p. 10, 2011b) has, that "critical thinking is reasonable and reflective thinking focused on deciding what to believe and what to do."

Deciding what to do and what to believe requires that students analyze the structure of competing arguments. To analyze competing arguments students must grasp which ones might reasonably apply to the challenge at hand. This requires in part that higher-level thinkers pay attention to the arguments and viewpoints of others. Attention to the arguments and viewpoints of others underscores that learning to become a critical thinker is truly a matter entering community with others. In this case that community constitutes something explained at length in chapter 2 as the community of the Great Conversation of Humankind.

A person may be better or worse at thinking about some matters as opposed to thinking about other matters. Personal thinking excellence varies with the subject matter under consideration, when it is considered, and even the mood and emotional stability of the thinker at the moment of cognitive challenge. At various times students may be more alert and astute at critical thinking and at other times be found somewhat wanting. This is no different than it is for adult thinkers.

In either case, success is as easy to explain as Joe DiMaggio explained success to a young boy who asked him, "Mr. DiMaggio, how do you get to Yankee Stadium?" DiMaggio famously replied, "It's easy kid. Just practice, practice, practice." And so it is with becoming a better thinker and getting into the midst of the Great Conversation: practice, practice, practice.

The American Philosophical Association (APA) Delphi Project did a good job of summing up what a thinker looks like when he or she becomes a major league critical thinker. The ideal critical thinker is habitually inquisitive, well-informed, trustful of reason, open-minded, flexible, fair-minded in evaluation, honest in facing personal biases, prudent in making judgments, willing to reconsider, clear about issues, orderly in complex matters, diligent in seeking relevant information, reasonable in the selection of criteria, focused in inquiry, and persistent in seeking results which are as precise and the subject and the circumstances of inquiry permit. (Facione, 1990, p. 2)

When a young man puts on that Yankee's uniform, he knows his practice has paid off. He is a major leaguer. He ascended the steps of Yankee Stadium. In critical thinking how does one know when one has ascended and taken one's rightful role amid the Great Conversation of Humankind?

Critical thinking programs should produce some evidence of thinking improvement. Improvement of thinking covers a lot of ground as is suggested in the APA statement. Like the major league baseball player who must exhibit appropriate dispositions such as self-discipline and mastery of many skills and excelling in a few, the critical thinker must similarly exhibit appropriate dispositions and mastery of many skills.

Even though better thinkers are especially skilled, those skills are not always recognized and prized by observers. In fact, it is not uncommon to hear the most incompetent thinkers declare themselves wise because they have what they call "common sense" or they are "street smart." These folks are usually quick to add that anyone who disagrees with them on this or that matter simply does not have common sense or is not street smart. Yet, as Faccione and Faccione (2013) underscore, the range of skills and dispositions of the major leaguer in critical thinking doesn't just happen. Excellence in thinking comes on the heels of instruction and much practice.

Nonetheless, true critical thinkers are not too quick to applaud their own talents and dismiss the ponderings of others. In fact, one of the traits of mature critical thinking is being disposed to listen to the arguments and viewpoints of others—all others—respectfully. That dispositional trait is central to admission into the Great Conversation of Humankind (Wagner & Lopez, 2013). There is of course more beyond this particular dispositional trait that can be observed in the development of critical thinking excellence appropriate for entrance to the Great Conversation.

To track how well various critical thinking programs approach ideal productivity, Faccione and Faccione (2013) developed two assessment instruments, namely the California Critical Thinking Dispositions Inventory (CCTDI) and the California Critical Thinking Skills Test (CCTST). Both of these instruments can be used effectively in monitoring critical thinking development in students. We encourage schools to consider the appropriate use of these instruments to monitor development of student skills.

Readers will find other resources described in a later section of the book. Also in the appendix the authors have provided directions to a website they maintain to respond to readers' queries about various resources in measurement tools, methodologies, and so on as needed.

BEING A CRITICAL THINKER

To engage in deliberative and reflective thinking is to become a distinctive sort of person (Kagan, 2016). It is to become a person who understands the importance of standards such as depth, clarity, and relevance. A deliberate and reflective thinker routinely applies the standards of critical thinking to social purposes and epistemic evaluations. In the process of routinely applying standards of critical thinking, the maturing minds of students increase in their autonomy and their ability to appreciate viewpoints of others (Cohen et al., 2006; Paul & Elder, 2011).

Practice in critical thinking is essential if one is to succeed as a critical thinker, and learning what to practice is part of the process of critical thinking itself. Some critical thinking skills are directly teachable, while others can only be picked up. Noting undefined terms and contradictions in lines of argument are skills that can be taught. Skills such as identifying key assumptions and noticing common fallacies are learned with guided practice. But becoming *alert* to unsubstantiated claims and the use of unclear terms can be learned but not exactly taught the way a skill is taught.

Together the skills that are taught and the dispositions that are learned make up a sort of mindware for developing critical thinkers (Nisbett, 2015). In an online article "Mindware and the Metacurriculum," David Perkins (2012) handily defines *mindware* as consisting in: "tools for the mind. A piece of mindware is anything a person can learn—a strategy, an attitude, a habit—that extends the person's general powers to think critically and creatively."

For students to fully participate in the Great Conversation they should develop increasing skill and appreciation for mindware such as logic, semantic analysis, statistics and probability, the design and conduct of experiments and field studies, game theory, and many other strategies that enhance a maturing mind's ability to think critically. These are also things that can be taught and should be taught (Gigerenzer, 2014; Rosenthal, 2014).

However, more than skills and tools are needed—students need to develop the dispositions that will situate them in the Great Conversation for a lifetime. Empirical research by the current authors, as well as by other scientific researchers, shows that students who experience structured dialogue about meaningful topics continue to think better than they would without that experience (Fair et al., 2015a, 2015b; Topping & Trickey, 2007a, 2007b). The commitment to embrace mindware is itself a disposition learned through participation in appropriately structured and successful dialogic events.

Evolution saw to it long ago that humans are natural learners. If students in our classrooms today seem unmotivated in their studies, that suggests something, we as educators or the surrounding learning ambience we foster, is unmotivating to students (Kagan, 2016). Quite possibly the drill-and-grill preparation for high-stakes testing, the isolation of computerized lessons, and the glibness of informational search technology may all play a role in discouraging students from developing their natural impulse to learn.

But the classroom learning ambience and the truth-seeking modeling of teachers and other classroom support staff can free the natural impulse for learning. Social psychologist Albert Bandura and many other educational psychologists have demonstrated the potency of incidental learning and role modeling (Bandura & Walters, 1963).

However, if educators fail to role model the life of inquiry, the ambience conducive to student practice in critical thinking will never be realized. If students are to continue to care about the quality of their thinking, then they will need to see teachers who care about truth-seeking inquiry, who show respect for the positions of others, who value clarity, accuracy, relevance, and all the other skills and dispositions we have mentioned in this chapter.

Certainly others like Gardner (1983), Noddings (1968), Paul (1985), and Perkins (2012) have made important contributions to help students learn to think more effectively. Familiarity with these approaches is optimal for a robust approach to teaching critical thinking and bringing students into engagement with the Great Conversation of Humankind. And, while scientists know much about critical thinking, there is still much to learn.

Nonetheless, there are sufficient resources to get every classroom teacher into a skill set that is more effective for developing in students' critical thinking now, and that is the task we address immediately ahead in the following chapters. After we explore some of those resources in the next three chapters, we will share hands-on scripts that are ready for immediate classroom implementation. These scripts are tools that can be used in various curriculums, from STEM to the humanities, from the arts to character development.

Structured dialogues about meaningful topics foster skills and dispositions of higher-level thinking. This book not only explains about the elements of mindware in the curriculum, but it also provides tools that accelerate students' acquisition of that relevant mindware. The structured dialogues that the scripts prompt are valuable to the extent that they sustain students' motivation as truth seekers who value understanding the world, themselves, and the viewpoints of others. The necessary mindware and dispositions can be summed up as focused on an ideal that recognizes that persistent doubt rescues the authentic truth seeker from intellectual complacency.

Chapter 2

Philosophical Inquiry and the Great Conversation

Bringing the Classroom Home to the Philosophical Crossroads

Philosophy sits at the crossroads of all other disciplines. If you ask ever deeper questions of physics, theology, mathematics, electrical engineering, social and political affairs, linguistics, musical composition, the meaning of humor, how best to get along with your neighbor, and so on, you inevitably find yourself face to face with philosophical issues and doing philosophy. The questions are inevitable and unavoidable. Whether or not one addresses them in a thoughtful manner is not inevitable. And whether or not one addresses them in a reasonable and clear-headed way is *too often avoided!*

John Dewey and later Matthew Lipman wanted to bring students to the philosophical crossroads early and often. Lipman was the pioneer who single-handedly brought philosophy into North American public schools. He spoke of wonderment and children's natural passion for truth. He spoke less of rigorous review and critical thinking, although clearly these are central to his initiatives since they are central to philosophy itself.

Lipman's initial foray into philosophy for children centered on creating a child's novel with a Jewish Aristotle as the protagonist. Lipman (1971) loved plays on words, and so his first children's novel was titled *Harry Stottlemeier's Discovery*. Say the title over a few times and you will hear yourself saying "Aristotle." Lipman's Harry is a twentieth-century boy wondering and critically reviewing his thinking, just as the philosopher Aristotle did many centuries ago in ancient Greece.

As Lipman's approach gained credibility, other initiatives in public school philosophy were attempted throughout the United States and also in Europe, Australia, and South America. As Lipman expanded his work across national borders, he also extended his curriculum by creating a series of children's novels to go with *Harry*. The novels covered the span from third grade to high school. To distinguish his approach from others, Lipman, on the advice of Paul Wagner, one of this book's authors, branded his program "Philosophy for Children" (P4C).

For Lipman's approach to work, a portion of the curriculum had to be dedicated to the sequenced set of novels Lipman wrote. The novels were to lead children directly to the crossroads of the various disciplines where philosophy reigns supreme and the foundations of various disciplines become alive through the personalities in the stories.

When Lipman's program worked, it worked very well. Unfortunately, in an age of high-stakes testing there was decreasing likelihood of schools segmenting off a piece of curriculum to be dedicated to P4C. Schools that kept Lipman's programs more often than not relegated them to the school's gifted program. The programs worked well there, of course, but the dream of Lipman and most other advocates of philosophy for children is that there be a rebirth of the evolutionary-given instinct for learning, wonderment, and critical review for all students, not for just a select few.

CHALLENGES OF CREATING A CLASSROOM AMBIENCE FOR PHILOSOPHY

If advocates of P4C insist that a whole segment of the standard curriculum be dedicated to P4C or some other philosophically based program, they are unlikely to get their foot in the door in an environment dominated by high-stakes testing and government-mandated core curricular standards. Unfortunately, by limiting opportunities for student philosophical engagement, it is the students who lose the most in the current standards-based environment.

Evolutionary psychology has made it abundantly clear that humans have a natural instinct to learn (Wiley, 2015). If students lose that instinct in public school, then something has gone dreadfully wrong. We believe teachers should be able to seize teachable moments at every opportunity and bring students again and again to the crossroads of the disciplines to ask big questions. These teachable moments can foster wonderment critical for sustaining students' natural instinct to learn.

When teachers are able to capitalize on these teachable moments and bring students into philosophical engagement with one another they open them to full participation in the Great Conversation of Humankind. Students need periodic opportunities for a rebirth of their natural instinct to question, ponder, and critically review claims to truth. Students need the intellectual dispositions and skills that will one day place them at the center of the Great Conversation of Humankind.

It is not important that something called "philosophy" works its way back into the curriculum. What is important is that "the Great Conversation of Humankind" permeates the classroom. Students deserve every opportunity to participate in that Conversation.

THE GREAT CONVERSATION

The term "the Great Conversation" is a handy way of designating the effort of human beings around the world to share their understanding of themselves, of others, and of the world itself. The Conversation is designated as "great" because it is about big questions that matter and that inevitably invite wonderment on the part of nearly everyone young and old.

For example, to wonder why conscience seems—sometimes—to restrict human action is a big question nearly every person asks at one time or another. Similarly, to wonder how humans ought best to organize themselves or to wonder how foods metabolize and produce energy are big questions prompting curiosity—given the right time and place. To wonder whether it is morally right for humans to eat other animals or to use a disproportionately large share of nature's bounty are similarly big questions relevant to all of humanity.

In contrast, to wonder whether I should order a fish sandwich or a burger for lunch is not a big question. No doubt many people ponder such questions and such questions may be important for personal health. Still individual dietary decisions are generally unlikely to rise to the heights of big questions suitable for analysis in the Great Conversation.

The Great Conversation is a *conversation* because it brings human minds together in a shared and collaborative search for truth (Wagner & Simpson, 2009). The Conversation takes place through journals, books, and various other media, as well as in the private ponderings of individuals and the collective dialogue of groups. While the Great Conversation may be the most inclusive of all human activities, there are, unfortunately, some individuals who are excluded because their education disabled their participation rather than enabling them.

When the Conversation takes place in the private ponderings of individual minds, it continues to use the tools of human language in a silent dialogue. Language by its very nature is public property. The words, terms, and sentences of human language are tokens of public intellectual commerce. No matter how silent human thinking is, its processes use concepts inherited from social engagement with other humans sharing thoughts (Tomasello, 2014).

THE ELEMENTS OF THE GREAT CONVERSATION

There is only one Great Conversation. That Conversation may have begun in numerous locations in Southern Africa, Central America, India, China, Greece, the Middle East, or the Far East. Most likely it began in some form in each of these places and other places besides (Mlodinow. 2014). Moreover, the Conversation continues all over the world wherever people do science, ask about the best forms of government or the nature of happiness and love, seek effective decision-making, and ponder all the questions that lead people to consider more robust ways of understanding the worlds within our minds and those worlds revealed by our senses.

One place where the Conversation took place early on is in Greece of antiquity. Two points make the Greek foray into the Conversation especially significant. First, Greek speculations into the operations of nature and its origins were extensively documented and handed down over the centuries.

Second, and more important, is the fact that the Greeks turned the Conversation in on itself. They did this by asking, first, what makes the Conversation great and, second, by asking how they can make the Conversation better. In other words they asked, "What does it mean to know?" "What do we mean by the term X?" and "What is the best way to structure an explanation?" They created logic, epistemology, metaphysics, ethics, and the roots of Western science.

The Conversation is great to the extent that it engages participants in mental life and in respectful communication with one another inclusively. The Conversation is also great to the extent that it leads to further understanding of its subject matter. And finally, the Conversation is great because it extends the individual autonomy of participants and their respect for other collaborators.

WONDERMENT AND THE SEARCH FOR TRUTH

Ironically, truth itself became a controversial topic within the Great Conversation. It is ironic that it would become a topic of the Conversation because in an important way truth is largely the point of the Conversation. Because the Conversation is open to all sincere inquiries that affect human existence, it is inevitable that the nature of truth itself became a topic of legitimate conversational interest.

In this treatment of the Great Conversation, truth is assigned the role of an ideal. *Truth is an accurate representation of matters as they are.* To speak the truth is to state matters as they are without evident error. To tell the truth is to state how things seem to be without any attempt at deceit.

Note the difference here as we move from ideal to practice. Truth tellers sincerely participate in the Conversation. Their aim is to get things right. As John Searle (1995; p. 49) declared, "the word 'true' indicates the aim." Aristotle asserted the matter a bit more confidently, "To say of what is that it is not, or of what is not that it is, is false, while to say of what is that it is, and of what is not that it is not, is true" (*Metaphysics* 1011b25). The Conversation cannot proceed without an acknowledged commitment to seek truth and to always make efforts to avoid error in the process of thinking.

The challenge is to ensure truthful representation at the conclusion of a successfully managed portion of the Great Conversation, and this is the domain of epistemology. Epistemology is the study of getting things right in our truth-seeking efforts. Here is where the Greeks most pointedly turned the Conversation in on itself. They made a concentrated effort to determine strategies for improving the Conversation's approach to the ideal of truth itself (Mlodinow, 2015). Epistemology and logic are as central to the Great Conversation today as they were in antiquity.

Today, for pedagogical purposes, epistemology and logic are typically conjoined under the term *critical thinking*. Keep in mind that using the term "critical thinking" in this fashion is quite generous. Epistemology and logic are now composed of numerous subdisciplines. The study of thinking has been enriched by studies in psychology and other social sciences, ranging from business, economics, decision theory, law, and applied mathematics (Binmore, 2009; Nitzan, 2010; Rachlin, 1989; Salsburg, 2001).

Furthermore, just as during the ancient Roman Empire people said all roads lead to Rome, all disciplines that focus on truth lead in the end to a crossroads, and that crossroads is philosophy. Thus, philosophy lies at the very heart of the Conversation.

It is easy to get overwhelmed by the breadth of the intellectual territory just crossed. However, the ambitions for what is to come are much more modest. The focus of this book is to show how to bring students from grades K through 12 into the Great Conversation. To do this, careful attention must be given to the levels of expected discourse and to topics appealing to the respective age groups. Moreover, the authors have focused on facilitating critical thinking in order to amplify the meaningfulness of the standard curriculum in each grade level.

The scripted topics in the chapters ahead are important not so much for their content as for the pedagogical invitation they present to students from differing grades and sociocultural backgrounds. It is the thinking skills and dispositional attitudes, those developed through participation in the dialogues the scripts prompt, that are keys to developing higher-level thinking within students. However, while higher-level thinking is often touted as important in public education, increasingly in practice, the focus has been away from the development of such skills and toward recognition dispositions instead (Ravitch, 2009).

RESTORING THE CONVERSATION

In the early 1970s, a small group of philosophers, including Paul Wagner, one of the authors of this book, began work on drawing elementary-age students into philosophic inquiry. The most noted of these individuals and the only one to begin to develop an extensive curriculum around philosophic inquiry was Matthew Lipman (2002). Many P4C and critical thinking projects, protocols, and practices followed. Unfortunately, however, these programs withered under the burden of oppressive high-stakes testing demands and uniform state and, most recently, national content standards.

No matter how successful individual critical thinking programs initially appeared, to the extent that they competed with curricula designed to prepare students for passing recognition items on high-stakes tests, the more likely they were to vanish. Advocates of critical thinking need to come to grips with the fact that it is unlikely that any well-organized public outcry is going to change the direction of events any time soon (Kohn, 2015).

Nonetheless, teachers committed to developing critical thinking skills, dispositions, and attitudes in their students need not give up hope. Instructional strategies for developing higher-level thinking skills in students can work even within the oppressive restrictions imposed by standardized curricula and measurement models (Kamenetz, 2015). Teachable moments may be fewer in number, but they do still occur, and in the chapters that follow there are practical exercises showing teachers how to make the best of those teachable moments for critical thinking.

A NOTE ON CRITICAL THINKING TO AVOID MISUNDERSTANDINGS

Before proceeding further, the reader needs to become mindful of some common preconceptions that distract people from understanding what critical thinking and philosophic inquiry are all about. Today, it seems we live in an overly politicized world. As a consequence, the term "critical thinking" is often associated with social revolutionaries and other adversaries of authority who have political agendas, favoring their own positions while discrediting those of others. This is not what critical thinking is all about. It is certainly not the sort of consideration that animates the work of the authors of this book.

As we have just indicated, critical thinking is not a matter of political allegiance. For this reason political issues are avoided in the scripts in this book. Certainly, critical thinking ought to make one better at thinking through complex political and social issues, but for pedagogical reasons the scripts in this book generally avoid tackling public policy issues. Moreover, since the intent of the scripts is to amplify the meaningfulness of much that is in the prescribed curriculum of the various states, there is little latitude for political controversy.

The term "philosophic inquiry" can be a distraction for some. Too many adults have a knee-jerk reaction to old jokes whenever the word "philosophy" is uttered. Many adults have heard the one: "Why does a philosopher always answer a question with a question?" Answer: "Why not?" Similarly, many have heard the legend of the philosopher who gave a test with one question, "Why?" and then rewarded a student with an "A" for answering "Why not?" These jokes are a bit silly, but they do contain an element of truth to the extent they suggest that questions drive philosophy.

Questions do drive philosophy. Questions also drive scientific advance. In fact, questions drive all critical thinking. Indeed, the two most potent questions include, "How do you know that?" and "What do you mean by X?"

Just as the question, "How do you know that?" drives effective critical thinking, the question, "What do you mean by X?" goes far to ensure that any advance in understanding is *shared*. Critical thinking is of little import if its results are not shared among earnest inquirers. Finally, attention to the question "What do you mean by X?" helps serious discussion from going down a rabbit hole. Serious discussion of any sort requires focus and not multitasking or inattention of any kind.

These two questions are so potent that one can argue that, if the Great Conversation were a tree, these questions are the cellulose fibers that give resiliency and structure to the tree. Branches, leaves, roots, and all the other parts of the tree play essential roles in keeping the tree alive, but the cellulose fibers give it structure and transport nutrients throughout the tree.

To press the analogy further, imagine the branches and leaves as hypotheses and the roots as definitions, assumptions, and background knowledge. And, just as sunlight, rain, and other nutrients bring about robust growth of a tree, these two questions nurture all the other questions of scholars and scientists. These two questions and their variants keep everyone very conscious about what they are calling knowledge and highly alert to the presence or absence of agreement on shared terms. In short, these questions sustain the robust growth of the Great Conversation.

THE IMPORTANCE OF SEMANTIC CLARITY

"Define your terms," the ancient Greeks demanded of one another. In contemporary times people may ask, "What do you mean by X?"—as President Clinton once did when he asked what his interrogators meant by the term "sexual relations." People scoffed at that, but in the context of a legal proceeding it was not an unreasonable request on his part. Some cynically declared he was using legalistic tricks to avoid answering pertinent questions, but that is not quite fair. People risk much in any conversation when they answer questions they think they understand but which are not, in fact, the ones asked.

It is always better for everyone involved if there is a meeting of minds between the questioner and respondent. Consider a greeting card showing an elderly woman approaching her husband in the next room. He is watching television with the sound blaring loudly. From behind him she asks, "Do you still love me dear?" He doesn't turn his head but says simply, "Sure. I'll have another beer." Now what just happened? Was the husband misunderstanding what his wife asked? Was he being cold in responding as he did and was sending an important subtext?

The fact is, we can never know from this information. We don't have enough to go on regarding what the husband thought he was being asked or what background information would lead the lady to interpret his response in one way rather than another. It would be intellectually irresponsible to speculate exactly what information was intended in the husband's response.

"What do you mean by the term X?" For participants in the Great Conversation or, for that matter in any conversation, there must be general agreement on the meaning of terms. Think again of Greek antiquity. Socrates incessantly asked alleged experts what they meant by important terms such as piety and justice. How can one know how to evaluate the assertions of anyone—including bona fide experts, unless there is a meeting of the minds on the meaning of key terms?

SITTING AT THE CROSSROAD OF THE GREAT CONVERSATION: SCOPE AND DIRECTION

We have mentioned science and mathematics often in discussing the role of critical thinking. But, as in the case of all roads leading to Rome, all sustained and full-blooded inquiries into the nature of critical thinking lead to philosophy at the crossroads of all the other disciplines. And because it is philosophy that sits at the crossroads, it should be no surprise that through philosophy, researchers construct grounds for research protocols and the justifiability of claims. Finally, no one should be surprised that matters of personal happiness and religion are also material for the Great Conversation.

Leading feminist educator Nel Noddings (1993) is certainly in sympathy with the broadly described scope of the Great Conversation when she writes in her book, *Educating for Intelligent Belief and Unbelief*, that discussions of religious commitment can foster critical thinking. Noddings reasons that this is true because the point of critical thinking is never to enslave or subordinate the opposition but rather to investigate.

Noddings is right. The commitment to seek accurate and shared understanding that guides the Great Conversation applies to religion, but there will be no religious scripts in this book. That is only because the subject-matter discussions we have selected for inclusion are more likely to have connection with the public school curriculum, including math and science studies (STEM) in particular.

The emphasis given to STEM studies is simply in recognition of the growing national interest in those studies in the curriculum. Moreover, since science and mathematics have a reputation for producing the most plausible accounts of reality, they serve most vividly as sources for critical review within the context of the Great Conversation.

In virtually every science there have been correlations noticed or even mathematically demonstrated, that did not prove any causal connections. Theories abound for these associations, but theories based on correlation must wait for stronger evidence to be amassed.

Waiting for stronger evidence is a consequence of attending responsibly to the "how do you know?" question. How evidence is to be determined to be optimally responsive to the "how do you know?" question is a concern that sits at the heart of the crossroads deep within the Great Conversation.

As a science matures, responses to the questions "How does that happen?" and "How do you know?" become more frequent, and they become increasingly plausible. Of course, these questions will never go away altogether. Add to these, questions concerning *why* things happen as they do, and it becomes apparent that the Great Conversation has an inexhaustible index of intellectual challenges for all participants.

CRITICAL THINKING AND LIVING BETTER WITH UNCERTAINTY

The Great Conversation invites everyone to consider questions of enormous theoretical impact, as well as questions of personal benefit. Answers to all these questions often require knowing how to extract enough information from science and observation in order to make prudent decisions. Such information is extracted from science through skillful and relentless employment of "how do you know?" questions.

Consider, for example, the situation facing women over fifty who are informed of suspicious shading in a mammogram. These women are routinely advised to undergo painful biopsy to check for cancer. The women are often frightened and ask doctors if this means they are likely to have cancer.

As Gerd Gigerenzer (2014) has pointed out, doctors acknowledge that they innocently tell women that mammograms detect 80 percent of breast cancers. With this information in hand, both women and doctors have a tendency to interpret a suspicious mammogram as indicating that a woman has an 80 percent chance of having cancer. Yet, this is far from the truth! Pressing the "how do you know?" question proves to be highly revealing.

The percentage numbers are not saying what patient and doctor imagine them to be saying. To see that this is so requires a bit of knowledge and thinking through the possibilities. First, you need to know the rate at which breast cancer occurs. If we focus one form of breast cancer, invasive cancer, the rate of incidence in women over fifty years of age is about 350 per 100,000 according to the National Cancer Institute.

Now assume that the mammogram sensitivity is such that it detects 80 percent of those who have cancer. That means that for about 280 of the 350 women who have the invasive breast cancer the test will give a *true positive* result; that is, it will correctly show that they have it. But it also means that 20 percent of the cancers, that is, seventy of the 350, will not be detected. Those women will receive *false negative* reports.

Now notice that if the rate of occurrence is 350 out of 100,000, for women over fifty, then the vast majority of such women, 99,650—thankfully!—do not have the invasive breast cancer. But the imperfect test that generates false negative results for some women will also generate *false positives*. The reported rate of false positives for mammograms is 10 percent. That means that when the 99,650 women who do *not* have the cancer are tested, the majority of them, 90 percent, will receive a *true negative* report. But nearly 10,000 (10 percent of 99,650 is 9,965) of them will receive a false positive report, indicating that they have the cancer when in fact they do not have it.

So if the test performs as we have assumed, then about 10,280 out of 100,000 women will receive a positive report. But the great majority of those positive reports will be false positives. Only 280 of the whole total of 10,280, that is, only about 3 percent will be true positives.

The problem of false positives is not an exclusively technological or medical issue for specialists. This all too common challenge takes us right to the heart of the disciplinary crossroads where statistics, biomedical research, and evaluations of risk aversion meet and critical thinking is imperative. Ordinary women, not just scientists, must make sense of what they are told in order to make competent decisions about what to do with their own bodies and how to manage the anxiety the information may cause.

Women need to figure out whether or not something is a dark and foreboding harbinger of things to come or something that can be addressed in a reasonably calm and systematic fashion. (As an example close to home, one of the authors of this book received a notice from his local blood bank that his blood tested positive for hepatitis C, but, because he knew about the high likelihood of it being a false positive, he could take the report in stride.)

The dispositions and critical thinking skills that come with participation in the Great Conversation are precisely those required for us to take control of our own lives, exercising autonomy where it most matters. Furthermore, even though it may seem remote, students considering choices ranging from the chance of acquiring sexually transmitted diseases to the chance of getting a suitably attractive partner for prom have their thinking improved by the same sort of analysis as in the women's mammogram dilemma (Wagner, 2013).

Gigerenzer, Lipman, and the current authors are of one mind and share a common ambition, namely, to bring critical thinking into the lives of students from the earliest age possible and foster a sense of autonomy in each of them. Then as adults, they can manage their own lives with greater success and they can enjoy a lifetime of inclusion in the benefits of the Great Conversation.

THINKING TOWARD THE BEST DECISION: ALLOWING FOR UNAVOIDABLE SURPRISES

Sometimes people learn when they reflect on the "how do you know?" question that we cannot close in on the ideal of truth in a given case. In such cases, people often still need to make a decision to act. In the end, everyone young and old, if they are to control their own destiny, must develop sound paths to the most plausible conclusion, paths that significantly improve their chances of realizing their individual and shared ambitions under conditions of uncertainty.

Ben Franklin famously opined that if a person wants to make the best choice regarding the selection of a wife, he should make a list of traits the various candidates have. The next step was to give these traits various weightings to reflect their importance in the potential suitor's mind. Finally, the suitor sums the positives and the negatives and supposedly selects the one with the best overall score.

But Franklin knew that one can never know for sure who will make the best wife. His methodology was intended to increase the odds that one might determine the best spouse out of the candidates available (Gigerenzer, 2014). Whether the question is addressed at seeking the best spouse or whom to ask to the eighth-grade dance, it is clear that there is no way of absolutely nailing down the truth of who the best choice is.

In making decisions in conditions of uncertainty, philosophers such as Paul Weinrich (2015), economists such as Richard Thaler (2015), and psychologists such as Amos Tversky and Daniel Kahneman (1986) are of one mind. Successful decision-makers must learn to accommodate uncertainty.

However, learning to accommodate uncertainty requires more than open mindedness, adaptability, or familiarity with statistics and formal logic. In cases of decision-making under conditions of uncertainty, it is not just a matter of chasing down missing information. There are often many reasons why uncertainty cannot be fully removed. One reason is that there may be too many considerations to weigh and sum up as Franklin advises.

A second problem is that under conditions of uncertainty, circumstances may drastically change on a dime. Nassim Taleb (2007), quantitative financial analyst by training and philosopher by temperament, calls these sudden shifts in problem framing "black swans." Black swans are abrupt changes that call for immediate action. He cites the events of 9/11 as an example.

By definition there are no available analyses to help people anticipate black swans. However, there is way to prepare for them. Developing the skills of reflective reasoning and the dispositions to employ useful heuristics and formal decision-making skills give people their best chance to cope when addressing sudden distortions of pattern. These skills and dispositions are higher-level thinking skills, and it is just these sorts of skills that we aim to develop in students through the use of scripted discussions.

THINKING TOWARD THE BEST DECISION: RECOGNIZING THE ROLE OF GUT FEELINGS AND INTUITION

The first person to consider a broad template of good thinking related to the work included in this book is Blaise Pascal. Pascal, in addition to being a scientist, a mathematician, and a philosopher, is perhaps most prominently known, if one is to count recent citations in business, economics, and psychology journals, as the father of decision theory (Hacking, 1990). Pascal was an exacting thinker. Yet, despite his mathematical skills as a pioneer in probability thinking, scientific reasoning, and decision-making under uncertainty, Pascal also kept open a window to what Lipman would call *wonder*.

In thinking about matters resistant to formalized reasoning, Pascal famously opined, "The heart has its reasons which reason does not know" (*Pensées*, 1958/1670, No. 277). In other words, Pascal's advice, like that of most decision theorists today, is that a good thinker should frame the problem as best he or she can, but doing that is only part of the challenge. Human rationality is inevitably bounded (Simon, 1982).

At times one must rely on feeling, intuitions, and even gut instinct to augment the best our lists and decision charts can achieve (Gigerenzer, 2008; Nisbett, 2015). Truly good thinking takes account of all these things. From Pascal to Lipman and the psychologists Baron (2007) and Gigerenzer (2014) to the philosopher Ernest Sosa (2011), all recognize that apt performance in effective thinking must sustain a sense of wonderment and passion for truth and must embrace the practice of critical review one learns in the Great Conversation.

SCRIPTING A PATH TO THE HEART OF THE CONVERSATION

Learning to engage the world more effectively is often a matter of bringing together minds in shared, critical reflection. The scripts ahead develop critical thinking generally because they center on building consensus and then employing cognitive dissonance to lure participants to challenge their own initial approaches to problem assessment and solving. The scripts prompt attention to language ("What do you mean by X?") as well as reasoning effectively with probabilities (How do you know?), as explained by psychologists such as Gigerenzer (2014) and Baron (2007).

In a world of specialization, the scripts bring critical thinking and decision theory together under a common theme of good thinking. The scripts found in chapter 5 aim to advance student autonomy and intellectual development. Conceptually, we are not the first to consider these higher-level thinking skills and dispositions. Certainly Bloom, Lipman, Baron, Paul, Ennis, Sternberg, Perkins, and many others have played important roles in bringing these considerations into education. But, we may be among the first to draw on a comprehensive range of scholarly insights in order to produce tools that can be used on the spot in the classroom as teachable moments allow.

In one way or another the Great Conversation focuses always on some aspect of *approximating truth*. While truth may never be fully within a researcher's grasp, C.S. Peirce, the nineteenth-century American mathematician and philosopher, may have been right in suggesting good research takes scientists and scholars ever closer to truth (Peirce, 1878). One can always ask further, "How do you know?" One can always ask, "What do you mean by the term?"

Not only scholars and scientists, but also every person, young and old, can learn to make more potent decisions by getting into the habit of pursuing these questions. The scripts here have been fashioned to help teachers keep focusing on these two questions from many different angles. The reader will see again and again how skillful pursuit of these two questions gives participants in the Conversation an increasingly firm grip on what is at stake throughout the Conversation.

Chapter 3

Psychological Research and Theories on Thinking

In chapter 1 we made it clear that interest in developing critical thinking ranges across a broad swath of scholarly disciplines. Indeed, since the time of Socrates and Aristotle, scholars have developed theories of thinking excellence. In the past century or so scientists have designed empirical studies to lay bare the processes and development of effective thinking in a variety of practical and theoretical contexts. This chapter focuses on the psychological aspects of critical thinking, and what follows is a very brief history of psychological influences on critical thinking.

NINETEENTH-CENTURY AND EARLY TWENTIETH-CENTURY PSYCHOLOGICAL APPROACHES TO THINKING

In the nineteenth century, George Boole proposed that thinking was "symbol manipulation" (as cited in Dellarosa, 1988, p. 2). Shortly thereafter, two structuralists, Wundt and Titchener, used introspection (Dellarosa, 1988) to analyze complex experience into basic sensory images (Gilhooly, 1996). At about the same time, the Würzburg School contended that thinking is "in part unconscious and imageless, yet goal directed and processlike" (Dominowski & Bourne, 1994, p. 9).

In the early twentieth century, functionalists such as William James and John Dewey described thinking "as a dynamic stream of interacting events" (as cited in Dominowski & Bourne, 1994, p. 14). However, behaviorists such as John Watson objected to the functionalists, insisting instead that genuine scientific investigation should restrict itself solely to observable data. This restriction discredited the study of thinking. Anything that could not be observed did not exist or at least was irrelevant to scientific investigation. At best, Watson accepted, thinking as "subvocal speech" (Dellarosa, 1988, p. 7).

From the 1920s to the 1930s, the Gestalt school of psychology, including Wertheimer, Kohler, and Koffka, resurrected the study of thinking and laid the foundation for contemporary studies of problem solving (Evans, 1995). The Gestaltists contended that an "adequate explanation of intelligent behavior required reference to internal states and highly integrated cognitive structures" (Dellarosa, 1988, p. 8). In short, for the Gestaltists thinking was an active and constructive process whose operations could be explained.

L.S. Vygotsky's influence on the study of thinking followed a line of thought similar to that of the Gestaltists. According to Vygotsky, people develop cognitive processes beginning in childhood and maturing through adulthood as a result of participation in the community (as cited in Gredler, 2009).

Vygotsky's proposal gained further credibility over the years when it was shown that, even in infancy, thinking is tied to practical problem solving (Langford, 2005). And, during early childhood, thinking is bound to manipulatives or "external concrete stimuli" (Gredler, 2009, p. 7). Children are thinking in the early elementary grades, but their thinking focuses on the formation of "pre-concepts." Pre-concepts are conceptual tools that do not yet show that the thinker has a full understanding of anything abstract.

The full management of concepts becomes evident when the thinker can operationally execute a line of thinking to achieve some abstract purpose. The young child's relative lack of conscious awareness of what he or she is doing while thinking limits the child's realization of the full range of logical thinking skills (Gredler, 2012). During adolescence this limitation of conscious awareness and dependence on external concrete stimuli is transformed into "inner-reconstructed operations" (Gredler, 2009, p. 7).

These operations constitute an internal mastery of acquired abstraction, including synthesizing, comparing, and differentiating concepts, that are essential for higher mental functioning (Gredler, 2012). Thus, Vygotsky concludes, "the adolescent [now] understands reality, understands others, and understands him or herself" (as cited in Gredler, 2012, p. 124).

Teachers can facilitate students' cognitive development and thinking, but not so much through direct instruction. Rather, teachers function best as role models of good thinking. As Gredler (2009) concludes, teachers' modeling thinking skills prompts more effective student thinking in context-driven situations. Teacher role modeling is thus central to the idea behind the scripts we include in this book.

In the 1930s, neo-behaviorists, such as B.F. Skinner, broke from the traditional associative learning theory of Watson and other early behaviorists. Skinner (1968) focused on variant reinforcement schedules to shape verbal behavior, which he described as the embodiment of thinking.

According to Skinner, teachers should specify the steps involved in acquiring each new skill. Unfortunately, as Noam Chomsky (1959) demonstrated in his review of Skinner's *Verbal Behavior*, this approach simply cannot account for how children learn language. The learning of language involves the application of transformative and generative rules that seem hardwired in the child's neurology and are not learned as a function of reinforcement schedules of any kind (Pinker, 1997). Arguments dismissing behaviorism are echoed by Wegner and Gray (2016) in *The Mind Club*.

Other psychologists in the mid-twentieth century from various fields noted the limitations evident in neo-behaviorism. F.C. Bartlett (1950, p. 145), for example, showed that thinking is a high-level skill where "evidence is given and the essential character of the process is to move beyond this evidence." Moving beyond the evidence requires attention to systematic anticipation, analogy, "interpolation" or "extrapolation" or both at times. The use of scripts prompting epistemic justification, as described later, requires students to use these processes to refine their thinking skills.

Jean Piaget was another psychological scientist who rejected behaviorism. Piaget was a constructivist because his view was that we each must construct our knowledge, and his studies demonstrated a sequence of four stages of construction in our cognitive development. These stages account for a number of critical developments in intellectual reasoning throughout youth. Piaget labeled the four stages sensorimotor, preoperational, concrete operational, and formal operational.

Piaget's research showed that children's thinking became more logical/rational throughout the elementary grades, progressing to the preoperational stage and then, finally, to the concrete operational stage (Ormrod, 2015). In middle school and then high school students finally evolve into formal operational thinkers. A brief discussion of these stages and why they matter follows.

During the sensorimotor stage (birth to two years), children cannot think of objects that cannot be seen. Next, symbolic thought begins to develop during the preoperational stage (two to seven years). This means that children can imagine objects not immediately before them and think about them. Upon entering the concrete operational stage (seven to eleven years) children begin to reason by virtue of their "concrete" experiences, which suggests that children can now order objects not immediately seen by qualitative and conceptual categories, such as size, color, and gradients of various kinds.

Also at this stage, children begin to develop capabilities for deductive reasoning. Piaget notes that children's thinking becomes more logical throughout the elementary grades, which suggests that logical thinking is a by-product of successful passage through the preoperational and the concrete operational stages (Ormrod, 2015). Developmental studies by Wegner and Gray (2016) show that young children learn to understand how others might see the same world as the children do but see it differently from their own perspective. This developmental step of being able to consider others' cognitive viewpoints increases throughout the elementary grades.

Finally, in the formal operations stage (eleven years to adolescence) preadolescents and adolescents evolve capacities for more exhaustive abstract and moral thinking, as well as inductive reasoning (Ormrod, 2015). One note of caution in regard to the stages is that research in the 1980s indicated that Piaget both underestimated children's and overestimated adolescents' reasoning abilities on his conservation tasks (Siegler, 1991).

As mentioned above, it is not until middle school and high school that formal operational thinking begins to flourish in students. This development of formal operational reasoning enables adolescents to solve abstract and hypothetical problems (Inhelder & Piaget, 1958) necessary for good thinking. The reader will find that the sample scripts presented in this book are designed to facilitate transition in students from preoperational to formal operational skills in a manner fully consistent with Piaget's and other developmentalists' reasoning.

BLOOM'S TAXONOMY OF COGNITIVE OBJECTIVES

Higher-level stages of thinking can be sorted and evaluated using a systematic taxonomy of objectives like that originally developed by Bloom, Englehart, Furst, Hill, and Krathwohl (1956). Bloom's original taxonomy postulated six hierarchically organized objectives in the cognitive domain: (1) knowledge, (2) comprehension, (3) application, (4) analysis, (5) synthesis, and (6) evaluation.

This taxonomy was later revised by Anderson and Krathwohl (2001). The revision was intended to capture more fully the activity of thinking rather than focus on the thinking product. The corresponding six objectives in the revised taxonomy are (1) remember, (2) understand, (3) apply, (4) analyze, (5) evaluate, and (6) create (see table 3.1). The use of verbs instead of nouns reflects a more dynamic approach to educationally relevant objectives. In addition, when ordering the objectives in this way, they scale a range of mental activities from lower-order to higher-order thinking skills.

These cognitive objectives denote skills people can improve. Consequently, the pedagogical application of these objectives has immediate value for classroom use. For example, *remember* focuses attention on students' recognizing or recalling information, while *understand* addresses a student's ability to explain the meaning of new information or ideas.

In the same vein, *apply* addresses a student's use of acquired knowledge and skills. *Analyze* addresses a student's ability to break down concepts and information and to show how they relate to one another. *Evaluate* addresses

Table 3.1 Bloom's Taxonomy of Cognitive Objectives

Old Version	New Version	Sample Outcome Verb	Instructional Strategy
Evaluation	Create	Develop, design	Cooperative learning, writing
Synthesis	Evaluate	Appraise, argue	Critiquing, discussions
Analysis	Analyze	Compare, question	Debates, hypothetical scenarios
Application	Apply	Demonstrate, solve	Case studies, authentic problems
Comprehension	Understand	Discuss, explain	Summarize, graphic organizers
Knowledge	Remember	Define, recall	Mnemonics, flash cards

Bloom et al. (1956), Anderson & Krathwohl (2001)

student ability to determine the merit of a line of thinking when given specific knowledge and criteria. *Create* addresses student abilities to develop a novel idea(s) or product(s) (Reeves, 2011).

Much research has supported the hierarchical nature of the first four original outcomes. However, as Huitt (2011) notes, research regarding the hierarchical nature of *synthesis* and *evaluation* from the original taxonomy is mixed. Huitt proposes that *evaluating* corresponds to what is generally described as critical thinking, because *synthesizing* and *evaluating* entail justifying a decision by using specific criteria or general epistemic standards. Thus, *synthesizing* and *evaluating* are a matter of students learning to master logical validation, that is, critical thinking. (See also Anderson & Krathwohl, 2001, for a more detailed description of the revised objectives.)

LATER TWENTIETH-CENTURY CONTRIBUTIONS OF PSYCHOLOGY

In the late 1950s and early 1960s the introduction of computers focused research on thinking as information processing. For example, Newell, Shaw, and Simon's (1958) theory of thinking postulated that human beings are information processing systems. That is, both humans and computers think by manipulating symbols in a rule-governed fashion.

The reader can see why we began this chapter with George Boole's claim nearly a hundred years earlier that thinking was a matter of skillful manipulation of symbols. As Boole anticipated, the central claim of information processing theory is that "cognitive processes and thinking can be described as a sequence of states each defined by a limited amount of information active in attention. . . . Each state provides the necessary input for the access of generation of information in the following state" (as cited in Dellarosa, 1988, p. 46).

Information processing models generally proposed three memory stores: sensory, short-term/working memory, and long-term memory. Each memory store varies as to how much information it can hold and for how long. That is, sensory memory has the least capacity for information. Short-term memory holds more data and for longer periods, but must "work" (e.g., chunking), at it in order to not to forget the information. Finally, long-term memory has an inexhaustible capacity for information retrieval. The interaction of these systems constitutes much of the cognitive aspects of thinking.

Jerome Bruner (1961), in considering information processing theory, found that "aspects of thinking can be conceived of as planful strategies designed to gain and organize information while at the same time regulating the risks of failure and the strains of overload brought about by man's highly limited capacity for processing information at any given moment of time" (p. 22). This organization of information is imperative for developing judgment, memory, problem solving, inventive thinking, and aesthetic skills (Bruner et al., 1956). Note how similar this is to the last two stages of Bloom's taxonomy.

Newer variations of the information processing model, such as connectionism, focus greater attention on how the retrieval of information from storage composes what we have historically described as thinking. Connectionism proposes that thinking involves substantial parallel processing when knowledge is coded and is distributed in one's brain (Bowers, 2002; Gilhooly, 1996). That is, there are multiple channels of thinking going on simultaneously in any thinker's mind and at any time.

According to McLeod, Plunkett, and Rolls (1998), connectionism implies that "there is no one place where a particular piece of knowledge can be located" (p. 31). Rummelhart, Smolensky, McClelland, and Hinton (1986) acknowledge that thinking comprises several sequences of brain states that fit the parallel processing model. They contend that these sequences are stable and reliably trigger underlying schemes of relevant components of knowledge (Gilhooly, 1996; Grossberg, 1999). This processing constitutes both learning and figuring things out for oneself (Grossberg, 1999).

In short, since the 1960s, the study of cognitive processes and cognitive development has led to a clearer comprehension of how humans think, how that thinking develops, and how humans might learn to think even more effectively (Nummedal & Halpern, 1995).

These new models of thinking, in conjunction with centuries of philosophizing about thinking, led to efforts to bring many insights into robust new practices for improving K–12 classroom instruction in effective thinking. Hence, in the early 1980s the critical thinking movement gained momentum by combining research and theories from psychology, philosophy, education, and most recently economics and decision theory. In fact, the coauthors of this book represent each of these fields of study.

Dissatisfaction among educators with the "back-to-basics" trend in education added further impetus to new research-based work in critical thinking (Martin, 1994). This, in turn, also prompted further interest in applying information processing and other contemporary models of natural and optimal modes of thinking to classroom learning and skills-based curriculums (Ericsson & Hastie, 1994).

Diane Halpern in the 1990s maintained that "teaching young children critical thinking skills lays the foundation for further intellectual development" (as cited in Murray, 1997, p. 5). Thus, when more effective thinking skills are learned through employment of new insights from the cognitive sciences, students can more truly master other subject-based topics.

Also, as Sigel (as cited in Bederson, 1990) notes, the emerging materials designed to teach thinking skills are intended to be developmentally appropriate for the age of the student. Again the reader can see here how the vision of Boole and the research of Piaget, Vygotsky, Bloom, and other branches of cognitive science are converging on an endorsement of teaching students better thinking operations.

An important additional note stressed by Howard Gardner (1990) was that a robust picture of mental life must include *cognitive emotions* such as surprise and wonderment. These emotions involve judgment and affect decision-making in proportion to the intensity of the respective emotion (p. viii). This idea originated with Israel Scheffler (1977), and it was further developed by Paul Wagner (1990) explicitly in the context addressed by Gardner.

CONTEMPORARY PSYCHOLOGICAL THEORIES

Jonathan Baron and David Perkins

One approach to the new thinking curriculums comes from the work of Jonathan Baron, who stated in functionalist fashion that good thinking (what we are calling critical thinking) is "thinking that achieves its ends" (as cited in Perkins, Jay, & Tishman, 1993). Baron's (1985) approach identifies two basic functions of thinking: gathering evidence and using evidence to solve problems, and he addresses mental events such as decisions, beliefs, and goals, "including decisions about what beliefs to believe and what goals to pursue" (Perkins et al., 1993; p. 68).

The scripts in this book reflect Baron's (1985, 2007) concerns since they aim at developing students' ability to make decisions *about* their beliefs and *about* what goals to pursue. We contend that some objectives of good thinking can be taught, namely attitudes, beliefs, and goals, but other aspects, such as dispositional habits and heuristics, are best learned in specific contexts. And we agree with Baron that teachers serve both as role models and as facilitators of thinking excellence. The scripts we share with the reader have been used in educational settings to accomplish both these objectives.

According to David Perkins and his colleagues (1993), there is no single process of thinking. This reflects the general position of many researchers in the cognitive and neurosciences. Perkins et al. (1993) describe "mindware," as a collection of diverse mental resources "coalescing" around a situation attracting students' immediate attention (p. 77). The resources of mindware include rules, procedures, and strategies that Perkins and later researchers such as Stanovich (2009) contend "must be retrieved from memory to think rationally" (p. 37).

More boldly, Stanovich declares that a "mindware gap" occurs when this knowledge is absent or otherwise unavailable (p. 37). Assessment and evaluation of specific situations are influenced by cultural knowledge (Perkins et al., 1993). We suggest that these enculturated assessments and evaluations tend to coalesce several elements of mindware under the guidance of a competent teacher and a properly guided discussion format. Again, the scripts in this book go far to develop the mindware resources Perkins and Stanovich seem to have in mind.

Robert Sternberg and Thinking Styles

Thinking styles is a concept developed by Robert Sternberg (1994; 1997b). For Sternberg (2003), a thinking style is a "preference for using abilities in certain ways" (p. 67). Basically, it is a dispositional tendency to employ elements of "mindware" in predictable ways. A *thinking* style is different from a *learning* style. That is, a thinking style pertains to the executive management of learned facts, heuristics, cognitive policies, and protocols. In contrast, "learning styles" for Sternberg denote dispositional patterns of acquiring information and categorizing knowledge.

Thinking styles are also interdisciplinary and can vary across individual tasks and specific situations (Sternberg, Grigorenko, & Zhang, 2008). To Sternberg (2003), thinking styles (as seen in table 3.2) are constructs that can predict school performance reflected in student grades over time.

Furthermore, thinking styles can be learned and assessed in various ways. Sternberg argues that, in the absence of special attention to thinking styles, "we may give the best grades to students who will later not be particularly successful in a given field, and derail other students who might be very successful but will never have the chance to prove it because of low course grades" (p. 69). Sternberg's point here is that grading only content acquisition can be very misleading as a predictor of student success beyond the classroom. Thinking styles must be taken into account if we are to remedy this situation.

Sternberg (1997a) notes also that the development of thinking styles is affected by several variables, for example, gender. In the past, the *legislative* thinking style was utilized more effectively in males than in females. Sternberg indicates that this association of gender and legislative thinking style is changing, but young girls are still socialized more often into the *executive* thinking style of "doing what they are told to do" (p. 30).

Another association is between age and thinking style. Sternberg maintains that, in preschool children, the legislative style is typically fostered in contexts that welcome creativity. However, elementary school children are encouraged to develop the executive thinking style because they are often simply told what to do. Using scripts is likely to promote legislative styles of thinking for boys and girls because they foster personal responsibility in reasoning. In addition, allowing children ownership of their own reasoning processes enhances their sense of wonderment, so critical to their creativity.

Sternberg (2003) uses concepts from conventional ideas of government as metaphors for his taxonomy of thinking styles. Governmental practices, he believes, are "external reflections of what goes on in people's minds" (Sternberg, 1997a, p. 20). Hence, he refers to his taxonomy as the "Theory of Mental Self-Government." This theory illustrates that "people can be understood in terms of the functions, forms, levels, scope, and leanings of government" (Sternberg, 2003, p. 72), which are depicted in table 3.2. (See Fasko, 2003, for a more detailed description of thinking styles.)

The forms of government are, in effect, indicators for human styles of organizing, governing, and managing themselves (Grigorenko & Sternberg, 1997; Sternberg & Zhang, 2005). The parallels between Sternberg's Theory of Mental Government and the revised Taxonomy of Cognitive Objectives are transparent, and both ideas support the utilization of scripted discussions in creating and sustaining communities of inquiry in K–12 classrooms.

Sternberg and Grigorenko (1995) further explain that people can use one thinking style but may change to a different thinking style as the context changes. Thus, "some individuals might be liberal in almost any situation, whereas other individuals might be liberal in certain kinds of situations but conservative in others" (p. 204).

Understanding thinking styles assists teachers in selection of discussion scripts when the intended learning outcomes focus student attention on reflective evaluation and synthesis (Sternberg & Grigorenko, 1995). For other learning outcomes, Sternberg (2003) and Sternberg and Zhang (2005) offer a number of suggestions for a variety of instructional types they see as well suited to different thinking styles given different pedagogical objectives, some of which are reflected in table 3.2.

Table 3.2 Thinking Styles in the Theory of Mental Self-Government

Thinking Style	Domain	Preferred Tasks and Situations	Method of Instruction
	Functions		
Legislative		That require creativity	Thought-based questioning, projects
Executive		That provide structure	Lecture, problem solving of given problems, Small-group recitation, for details and main ideas, memorization
	Forms		
Judicial		That requires evaluation	Thought-based questioning, small-group discussion, for analysis
Monarchic		That lets one focus on one idea	
Hierarchic		That lets one multi-task within a time-frame	Lecture, reading
Oligarchic		That lets one work with competing methods	
Anarchic		That allows one to be flexible	
	Levels		
Global		That allows one to work with big, abstract ideas	For main ideas
Local		That focus on specific concrete elements	For details, memorization
	Scope		
Internal		That allows one to work independently	Reading
External		That allows one to work with groups	Cooperative learning, small-group recitation and discussion
	Leaning		
Liberal		That provides new challenges	
Conservative		That are well defined	Memorization

Note. Adapted from Sternberg, R. J. (2003). Thinking Styles. In D. Fasko (Ed.), *Critical thinking and reasoning. Current research, theory, and practice* (pp. 74–75). Cresskill, NJ: Hampton.

Sternberg (1997b, 2003) suggests that the use of specific questions stimulates individuating thinking styles on the part of students. For example, asking students to "describe" something may prompt the use of the *executive* thinking style, whereas asking students to "compare and contrast" or "critique" may prompt the use of a *judicial* thinking style.

The questions so frequently encountered in our scripts, which ask students to "create," "imagine," and "suppose," prompt the use of the *legislative* style of thinking. Sternberg (2003) insists that teachers can balance the needs of both students and the assigned curriculums by encouraging students to use a variety of thinking styles as appropriate to the cognitive challenge.

Daniel Kahneman: System 1 Thinking and System 2 Thinking

Closely related to thinking styles is the idea of heuristics. Heuristics are thinking strategies that are fast and often reliable in daily contexts in which people most often rely on them. However, cognitive scientists have shown that heuristic tools applied in many contexts can be highly misleading when they are applied in situations calling for more deliberative and reflective thought.

On the flip side, research also suggests that people who have a better comprehension of the applicability of three common heuristics, namely representativeness, availability, and anchoring, can make better judgments and decisions in "situations of uncertainty" (Tversky & Kahneman, 1974, p. 1131; see also Kahneman, 2011, for a more detailed description of these heuristics).

When solving problems, Kahneman (2011) suggests being aware of fast or System 1 thinking and slow or System 2 thinking. System 2 thinking is more analytical, and it monitors System 1. The slow System 2 thinking is required in situations of deep abstraction and complexity. In contrast, the relatively fast thinking of System 1 employs heuristics and other readily available intuitions to reach decisions readily when urgency is required or the level of complexity is minimal.

In short, when "entirely automatic mental activities of perception and memory" (p. 13) are sufficient to address a cognitive challenge, fast thinking is natural and effective in most contexts. Admittedly, heuristics and other intuitions are especially vulnerable to bias. Nonetheless, when "experts have learned to recognize familiar elements in a new situation," heuristic thinking is appropriate (Kahneman, 2011, p. 12).

Thinking would not be productive if it were routinely riddled with bias. This problem is not easily avoided for, as Kahneman (2011) says about System 1, it "is not readily educable" (p. 417). People must be trained to avoid bias and misapplication of fast thinking practices. Kahneman suggests that "the way to block errors that originate in System 1 is simple in principle; recognize the signs that you are in a cognitive minefield, slow down, and ask for reinforcement from System 2" (p. 417).

The scripts developed for this book make extensive use of the concept of conceptual minefield. The scripts deliberately lure discussion participants into an easy and readily promising conclusion only to surprise them with paradoxes and other unacceptable consequences of their premature commitments. This strategy of scripting is deliberately in line with the recommendation Kahneman has long espoused, namely to teach people to allow slow thinking to actively monitor the sometimes inept performance of fast thinking.

Here we find the notions of the cognitivist Kahneman and the epistemologist Ernst Sosa (2015) in alignment. Each recognizes that thinking is a *performance*. It is a performance that can be done well or not so well. When slow thinking is required, the performance requires much greater skill and exactness of consideration to overcome fast thinking habits. There are conceptual "landmines" in the scripts in order to halt reckless fast thinking. The unwary thinker who wanders into a field of landmines learns quickly how to retrace one's steps and to think through a problem in a more measured fashion.

The scripts serve pointedly to bring people from the inappropriate use of fast thinking to the more demanding task of slow thinking. Clearly, the slow thinking our scripts produce and that Kahneman (2011) advocates developing in students is the heart of critical thinking.

Keith Stanovich

As noted above, bias is a contaminant of critical thinking. Bias is often unintentional and simply influenced by innocently acquired prior beliefs (Stanovich & West, 1997). To avoid bias, Stanovich (2009) explains that it is imperative for people to be trained to search for falsifying evidence. Again, the scripts' conceptual landmines are intended to alert people to unwitting biases they may have acquired. Repeated exposure to the cognitive dissonance our scripted landmines create leads to greater alertness in the performance of slow thinking and the need to search for falsifying evidence to avoid bias.

When students are exposed to flaws in their fast thinking as a result of encountering paradox or falsifying evidence in a script, they are generally able to see the value of more rational, slower deliberation. They see the value in deliberative thinking to the extent that they recognize slow thinking gives them a more accurate picture of reality (Stanovich, West, & Toplak, 2012).

SO WHERE DO WE GO FROM HERE?

In general, psychology has taken the lead in demonstrating that intellectual skills, critical thinking, and the effective reflection which advances the Great Conversation of Humankind can all be developed through a variety of strategies. The identification of reflective thinking skills in the 1960s along with programs in philosophy for children, as well as other critical thinking programs for K–12 students added a promising new dimension to education that has yet to be fully realized in practice.

The next chapter explains how the scripted discussions in this book utilize the knowledge of critical thinking pedagogy to place practical exercises into the hands of teachers. The exercises are designed to take advantage of the rare teaching moment. They are not a substitute for curriculums that are already overburdened with content and testing.

As we proceed, the utility of the scripted exercises and the advice in the very last chapter for developing one's own curricular materials will become increasingly easy to understand. Importantly too, the strategies of scripted discussions are liable to excite teachers at the very real opportunity they have to bring students of every age into the Great Conversation of Humankind.

Chapter 4

Establishing a Community of Inquiry in the Classroom

CREATING COMMUNITIES OF INQUIRY: A NATURAL THING FOR HUMAN BEINGS TO DO

Human beings are herd animals. This means that like gazelles, lions, coyotes, sheep, ants, bees, schools of fish, and gaggles of geese, evolution has preserved the species through adaptations of signaling equipping humans for cooperative engagements with one another (Wiley, 2015). As Martin Nowak, a mathematical biologist, along with a host of psychologists has pointed out, humans have become evolution's "supercooperators" (Nowak & Highfield, 2012; Pfaff, 2015).

Human cooperativeness gives rise to things like promises, property, and the transfer of goods over time across generations and across all geographic borders. The turning point, catapulting human cooperativeness far beyond anything evident in any other species, was the co-development of language and the social institution of the promise.

Certainly even the most cursory review of the range of human language shows that today language use goes beyond anything the species needs for survival. Humans speculate about infinity and even about different sizes of infinity. These speculations neither raise food for sharing nor do they bake bread. They are of no immediate practical utility on a day-to-day basis. More astonishing perhaps is the fact that infinities are outside anything humans have ever directly experienced.

In addition, through language use, humans share worries about what is truly beautiful, about what is really right or wrong, and about romance and love. Look to other social animals and you will see that such considerations as these are nowhere in evidence. Other animals are attracted to one another, are curious about objects of various kinds, and are mindful of status hierarchies.

These are all things necessary for reproduction and survival. But probing into topics like these is nowhere seen among other animals, perhaps because our language resources exceed anything observed in other animals.

The promise is the most extraordinary social device ever. All currency interactions are instances of promising. Weddings are obviously promising events, but so also are the collaborative efforts of scientists, engineers, politicians, medical teams, sports teams, and so many other groups since the members tacitly or explicitly agree to work together, all the while accepting self-imposed constraints as part of the deal.

In short, with language in hand and with all the moral commitments that accompany promising, evolution created the conditions of modern human communities and, more to our purpose, the conditions for communities of truth-seeking inquiry. Humans have used this set of linguistic and social tools to turn a rudimentary community of inquiry into the stunning Great Conversation of Humankind in which individuals who are prepared can participate.

The general features of the Great Conversation are, first, a focus on truth and not just what might get one or another person through the day. Second, through the Great Conversation humans try to know more. More important perhaps is the fact that through the Great Conversation, humans try to ensure that they know that they know more.

Third, in the Great Conversation every fellow truth seeker is welcome lest something important be overlooked if any collegial truth seeker is excluded. Because truth is the ideal, critical thinking and a healthy dose of skepticism pervade every genuine instance of the Great Conversation. There is no room in the Conversation for prejudice of any kind. This, in turn, means respect for each participant is a must.

While everyone is welcome into the Great Conversation and while it is the desire of this book to show ways for bringing students into it, we should be aware that moments of the Conversation are not always as common as would optimally benefit both individuals and the communities of which they are apart. People engage in many conversations. Sometimes they engage in conversation simply to propagandize and manipulate one another. Such conversations are never instances of the Great Conversation.

Sometimes people engage in conversation to deal with the immediate and mundane: "Jane, do you know where I left my keys?" "You are always losing your keys. Why don't you be more careful?" Searching for one's keys is important, but it does not normally lead one to consider the grand questions that the big brains of humans are especially talented at exploring.

In the Great Conversation the questions at hand are always focused on deeper insight and the self-correcting review questions like "How do you know?" and "What do you mean by that term?" make possible. In the Great Conversation people explore the nature of the universe, why is there something rather than nothing, what is happiness, what is love, or what is the best form of government. Whenever people delve into deep matters with an open mind and welcome constructive criticism, they are engaged in a moment of the Great Conversation.

You are participating in the Great Conversation simply by reading this book thoughtfully, when you began to contemplate how the curriculum ought to be and what teaching strategies ought to accompany it. We proposed when considering such matters, to focus on the centrality of critical thinking skills and dispositions, all with an eye to apprehending truth.

In chapter 2, you learned that if you ask questions about anything deeply enough, you will find yourself doing philosophy. Philosophy stands at the crossroads of all other disciplines. So when we think about developing a community of inquirers prepared for participation in the Great Conversation, it is inevitable that we start with philosophizing as the most natural way of beginning and sustaining progress in the Great Conversation.

Of course philosophers are no longer the only ones who craft suitable tools for participation in the Great Conversation, and so throughout this book you are referred to the work of psychologists, economists, decision theorists, statisticians, anthropologists, and scientists who have refined the skills and dispositions of successful participation in the Great Conversation.

Thus, in chapter 3, you learned more specifically what psychologists, economists, and other social scientists have learned about critical thinking and the dispositions that most effectively put these skills within reach of students being brought into the Conversation. Indeed, in recent decades, scientists have done much to identify the interactions of these skills and dispositions

Creating Communities of Inquiry: Necessary Skills and Dispositions

When creating a community of inquiry, teachers need to rely not only on the dispositions and skills of particular individuals, but also attention must be given to the skills and dispositions making up the intellectual ambience of the community. These skills and dispositions at both levels must come together in symbiotic fashion to optimize participation in the Great Conversation.

DISPOSITIONS OF INDIVIDUALS AND THE COMMUNITY

Individual Dispositions

It appears that evolution gave humans at least three aces for survival, each of which turns out to be relevant to participation in the Great Conversation.

One ace is the human propensity to be a social animal. As in the case of all other social animals this meant that humans tended to cling together. For survival, humans learned to work together and not in opposition to one another.

The second ace is a set of signaling practices that gradually evolved into language resources far out-stripping anything found previously in other social animals. This linguistic potency enabled humans to speculate and analyze. Humans are no longer attracted to one another simply for safety and procreation. Humans are learning how and why things happen through skilled public discussion. For example, beyond mere instinctual attraction humans now pursue questions about the nature of beauty and beauty making.

Instinctual tracking of resources led to counting and musing about geometries and infinities. The needs of cooperation led humans to theorize about concepts and practices of punishment and virtue. All of these transformations became possible because humans evolved a language that made such inquiries possible (Mlodinow, 2015; Wiley, 2015). This linguistic potency enables humans to speculate and analyze far beyond the known capacity of any other social animal (Pinker, 1994).

The last ace dealt to humans sometimes catches people in education off-guard. Teachers and many educational psychologists have spent much time and effort in the past 100 years trying to figure out how to motivate students, but with the advent of evolutionary psychology and other social sciences, it becomes increasingly evident that evolution made humans a natural learning species (Pinker, 1997). The central pedagogical question may well become not so much how should teachers motivate students but rather what is going on in the nation's classrooms that inhibits that natural motivation.

Think about it. How often have you stood in line at a grocery store and watched people read the tabloids by the checkout registers? How many times have you seen people at breakfast reading a newspaper, book, or even the back of a cereal box? Humans simply seem unable to stop themselves when it comes to learning (Gopnik, 2009). The brain evolved to seek out and accommodate stimuli. If students are not attentive to school curriculums, it may not be because their brains have shut down. Rather, students may simply be bored or have learned to shun what the system offers and daydream.

Together, these three aces make nearly every student a natural participant in a community of inquiry. However, for these evolutionary riches to be enjoyed by individual learners, there must be communities with a nurturing ambience for collective engagement to flourish (Henrich, 2015).

Community Dispositions

Evidently humans from a very early age on (contra Piaget) are fairly well equipped for entering into a community of inquiry. (The reader may recall that in chapter 3, it was noted that Piaget underestimated the preoperational child's cognitive abilities.) But they must be nurtured in the appropriate skills and dispositions in order for their natural capacities and inclinations to be realized. Children are given that nurturing when the community of inquiry they are entering is disposed to welcome novices.

Participation in a community of inquirers is not so different from participation in a community of hunter-gatherers. Each participant must be prepared to cooperate with other members of the community. It is clear that humans not only cooperate with one another, but they also ponder the importance of respecting one another as individuals and as members of families and other predisposing groups (Pinker, 1997). Most importantly, an imperative for any community of inquiry is that it fosters a sense of collegial respect for all who participate.

Another collective reason for creating a community of inquiry is that it prompts and sustains a sense of wonder among all who participate. It is one thing to wonder alone, but wonder is amplified in exciting ways when it is shared with others. In reviewing recent curriculums endorsing various instructional strategies, it seems that the "philosophy for children" approaches and the "discovery learning" approaches in science (Rakow, 1993) and social studies education have been particularly successful in developing a shared spirit of wonder among participants in their respective communities of inquiry.

A third imperative for creating a community of inquiry is that it impassions every participant's search for truth. One of the ways the community achieves this impassioned quest is by its leader's role modeling genuine truth seeking, and by gently disparaging the willingness to give up on a quest by simply settling for whatever seems good enough.

In creating the necessary ambience for a successful community of inquiry in the classroom, all the skills of pedagogy must be employed with a serious sense of purpose. That purpose is to develop in students a sense of autonomy and passion, so that they are always involved in keeping the Great Conversation alive and ever more fine-tuned.

SKILLS OF THE INDIVIDUAL AND OF THE COMMUNITY

Individual Skills

Dispositions and skills are different sorts of things. Dispositions move us to respond in particular ways when we are in certain conditions. Dispositions are more often than not learned through role modeling and participation in a favoring community. Skills, by contrast, are something most often taught and employed more deliberately through practice. Many psychologists recognize a distinction between mere cognitive activity and deliberative thinking. In fact, many social and cognitive psychologists today utilize Kahneman's (2011) distinction between "thinking fast" and "thinking slow."

Much fast thinking occurs subconsciously and uses culturally acquired patterns of thinking to quickly meet worldly demands. In contrast, slow thinking is more deliberate. Acquired dispositions enable people to distinguish between times and contexts when each type of thinking is most likely to lead to success. So, fast thinking directs us out of the way of an oncoming vehicle, but when the truth really matters we see the importance of slow and deliberative thinking. Slow thinking puts the brakes on and demands that skills of critical thinking be employed in order to secure the most plausible answer.

The slow thinking skills required for participation in The Great Conversation include being able to use terms precisely, with a degree of semantic exactness. These skills also include identifying and assembling assumptions in order to see the relevance of specific pieces of evidence. Finally, these skills must help students recognize the dependence of sound conclusions on plausible arguments. There is a difference between people simply offering opinions to one another instead of setting forth an argument or an explanation in a skillful attempt to secure a plausible conclusion.

The scripts teach semantic clarity within the context of the Great Conversation by persistently seeking ever more precise meanings of the words students use to explain their conclusions. The scripts teach logic by exposing students to what we call "landmines," thereby creating cognitive dissonance (Festinger, 1957). The scripts often evoke an initial consensus among students entering the discussion for the first time. However, the consensus is broken by presenting a question or description of an event that is in apparent conflict with much of what they have already asserted.

For example, a couple of scripts concern the concept of "beauty." In our culture there is a knee-jerk reaction to simply assume the truth of views that amount to "beauty is in the eye of the beholder." But this knee-jerk judgment is surely premature. And so it is time for students to encounter a "landmine." Consider that people pay more money for some art they find more beautiful than for other art. Students may be asked to consider as well that people contemplate what beauty is in the abstract apart from what individuals or their cultures may acknowledge as attractive.

And yet there is another landmine effect in drawing students' attention to the fact that people see themselves as looking truly beautiful one day and not so beautiful on other days. Not to mention other aesthetic facts such as some people may find a great variety of things beautiful like an act of kindness or a mathematical proof. Each of these cases raises a serious question about the validity of the knee-jerk response that beauty is, *as a matter of fact*, simply in the eye of individual beholders.

In the Great Conversation the point is not to simply rest content with each student's initial opinions. Rather all are encouraged to challenge those opinions in order in the end to create a conclusion that seems sufficiently plausible to other skillful thinkers. The point is to arrive at a situation where all, or nearly all, discussants can find grounds for common agreement and understanding—even when adopting on occasion disparate conclusions.

Community Skills

On almost any day in any large school, two types of discussions can be found, each of which discourages student learning and development into autonomous participation in the Great Conversation. The first type of discussion is one in which students are encouraged to participate, but only until someone arrives at "the right answer." In these discussions students quickly learn that there is no real seeking of truth by the community; rather, the discussion reduces to a guessing game, with each student trying to tag the answer the teacher was hiding all along.

The second type of discussion is one in which the teacher begins by announcing to the class, "There are no right or wrong answers to what we are about to discuss." Obviously, this simply serves to announce to the students that the activity they are about to embark upon is pointless. If there are no right or wrong answers, then there is no place for the discussion to go, no progress to be made. Educational psychologists such as Brophy and Good (1974) long ago disparaged both these approaches to classroom discussions.

At a presentation on the nature of truth to a group of science educators by one of this book's authors (Paul Wagner), an engineering department chair spoke up and told the science educators they needed to walk across campus sometime and meet with students in engineering. He told them that engineering students know when they get things wrong. Their buildings collapse, their bridges fall down, their nuclear reactors crack, and so on. Engineers do not have grand cosmic truths at their disposal, but they sure know a lot about what does not work, and they incorporate that knowledge in plans and arguments to construct things that are most likely to work.

This is as it is in the Great Conversation, generally. In contrast, if a teacher in a public school classroom announces there are no right and no wrong answers to a question, then she or he discredits the effort of students to participate before the discussion even begins. When we establish a community of inquiry, everything depends on the participants' sincere and passionate desire to search for truth and shared understanding.

The sense of wonderment that Philosophy for Children theorists and other champions of critical thinking advocate is predicated on the idea that there are worthy understandings of matters that can be sought and shared. Establishing a community of inquiry means that each participant acknowledges he or she does not know everything relevant to the topic at hand. It is a community of *inquiry* both because it seeks truth and because it remains forever gently and modestly skeptical of its conclusions.

In a community of inquirers it is understood that humans have inescapable fallibilities and Grand Truth is not in the offing. However, in any community of inquirers, who can lay claim to moments of the Great Conversation, there is a recognition that through communal effort participants have the ability to recognize some mistakes, set aside old prejudices, and ask new and challenging questions.

A skillful community of inquirers sets out hypotheses and various speculations for critical review. Those hypotheses and speculations that prove to be free of contradiction or are not in violation of the evidence can then be used as the basis for planned action at the moment and preserved for review in the future.

Constructing a Community of Inquiry in the Classroom

The process of creating a community that we are describing is strongly supported by empirical research (Fair et al., 2015a; Topping & Trickey, 2007). We have talked about dispositions that participants in the Great Conversation must have, and these dispositions manifest underlying values. These dispositional *values* form a moral architecture *that shapes and gives structure* for individual class discussion sessions (Wagner & Simpson, 2009). In the next few chapters, scripts designed specifically for upper elementary students give teachers content for those responsibly structured class discussions.

Dispositional Values for a Community of Inquiry

Creating a community of inquiry cannot be completed as the result of one successful class session. Rather a community emerges throughout the semester little by little. To make this happen, it is important that class discussion sessions happen as often as the mandated curriculum may allow. There is no magic here; the emerging community of inquiry simply unfolds when skillfully nurtured by teachers in an organic process that needs time to unfold (Cleghorn & Baudet, 2002; Lone, 2012; Lone & Burroughs, 2016; Paul & Elder, 2012; Wartenberg, 2009).

As noted previously, in a community of inquiry, students must learn the dispositional value to respect each participant. In addition, as noted above, each participant must recognize that an advance of understanding in the pursuit of truth could come from any participant, and so each participants needs to be listened to carefully. It is important to underscore here that *respect for each other as thinkers* is not shown by nodding in mindless agreement with what others say. To treat each other seriously as thinkers means that it is okay to question and even okay to challenge what is said.

Since the point of the Great Conversation is truth seeking, it is perfectly in order to ask for *greater clarity* about crucial concepts (What do you mean by that term?), to ask exactly how the speaker's comments are *relevant to* the question being discussed (How do you know?), to ask for *more specifics* to illustrate a speaker's point of view, to call attention to *implications* that accepting a proposed response to the question has for other situations, and to ask *what evidence or reasons* make the point of view seem to the speaker to be true—or at least closer to the truth—than alternative responses.

These dispositional values should become increasingly evident to the teacher as they take root and get stronger over time. As noted above, the community of inquiry comes into being step by step in the classroom over the semester, the school year, and the entire educational experience.

A Recommended Structure

To the extent that it becomes evident that the necessary moral architecture and ambience of the community of inquiry is developing, teachers may find they can accelerate its continued development by moving themselves a bit further back from the discussion by, after initial practice, having a student present the script. Having the student read the script after an appropriate ambience has already begun to develop in the community can help emphasize that this is *their discussion.* The teacher may only need to be present as a facilitator to keep things on track.

The idea is to enable every student to share his or her views. To this end, it may also be profitable to have students break into small groups with one student serving as the scripter in each. This gives further opportunity for shy and reticent students to participate. In any case, it needs to be clearly understood that *everyone* is expected to share what they are thinking, including any reasons they may have for their views.

In the next chapter are the scripts themselves. There is nothing iron clad about the upper elementary script designation. It may very well be that some of the scripts in this book could be used with older learners. And, scripts that might be designated as middle school or high school could be used with upper elementary students. Educators need to use the scripts appropriate for the learners in their classrooms.

The final chapter invites you to write your own scripts, and gives you some guidance on how to do it. The scripts we give you are helpful starting points, but after you reach a comfort level with the process and after the community of inquiry is well established in your classroom, there is no reason why you cannot introduce discussion prompts and scripts that you have selected or created with your students in mind.

Finally, in addition to the chapters, note the Resources section at the end of the book wherein we give you information to our website. We stand ready to assist you as you embark upon further adventures in scripting and critical thinking on your own.

Part II

SCRIPTS AND SCRIPTING

Tips for Using the Scripts Successfully

- **Read the entire script before reading it to your students.** This will help you know when you need a dramatic pause or a quick follow-up.
- **Be patient with your students.** Give them time to think. Many may have never had the opportunity before to think critically. These opportunities will help move them forward.
- **Never give your opinion.** Once you jump into the discussion with what you think, the "right" answer has been given, and student thinking and conversation will shut down.
- **Wait time.** Read the script/question and wait . . . quietly!
- **Use the scripts as often as possible.** Although there does not have to be a set curriculum or timeline, the more opportunities the students have to stop and think critically, the more improvements and risks you will see.
- **Make this time special.** Before beginning the scripts, have the students close their eyes and relax. This lets them know that something different is about to happen. It will seem silly at first but students quickly begin to enjoy this break.
- **Think, pair, share.** Sometimes students are more comfortable having time to write their ideas and sharing them with a partner or small group before sharing with the large group. This is true with difficult topics or when students are just beginning the process.
- **Fit the scripts in as an introduction to a lesson or when waiting in line.** There is no set time for critical thinking. You will find that some scripts will require a longer instructional time. Others are fun and can encourage your students to think critically while waiting for their turn in the restroom.
- **Reuse some of the scripts at the end of the school year.** This way you can really see the development of your students' thinking.

Chapter 5

Elementary Scripts

Students attending elementary school usually range in age from about seven to eleven years, and are typically in Piaget's Concrete Operational Stage of cognitive development. These students benefit from the opportunity to indulge in abstract and critical thinking and must be encouraged to do so.

The scripts in this section encourage elementary students to experience and practice abstract thinking. This practice can be the elementary student's first glimpse into the Great Conversation of Humankind.

BELIEFS

Are beliefs real? If you were to believe that George Washington is still president of the United States, you would be mistaken, right? Your belief would not be a piece of knowledge, right?

Is *knowledge* something different from *belief*? If I tell you I have a dollar in my pocket and you ask me how I *know* that I have a dollar, what can I do to show you I really know what I am talking about? I might pull the dollar from my pocket and show it to you. This would probably mean I knew what I was talking about when I said I knew I had a dollar in my pocket, right?

What would you say if I reached to pull the dollar out of my pocket, and I couldn't find one there? One thing you might say is that I really didn't know about the dollar. But certainly I did *believe* I had a dollar! I thought I was telling you the truth when I told you that I knew I had a dollar in my pocket. But, as it turns out, I had no dollar. So, I really didn't have the knowledge I thought I had, right? Did I have a real *belief* about having a dollar? What makes my *beliefs* real?

Let's pretend that you wanted to be helpful. You might laugh and say that I certainly didn't *know* that I had a dollar in my pocket, but then you suggest that I look in my desk for the dollar. Now, suppose I say, "No, I don't believe the dollar is there. I never put dollars in my desk." Nevertheless, you insist that I look, and when I do, I find my dollar! I didn't *believe* the dollar was in the desk, but it was! Were my beliefs about the dollar and desk real?

What kinds of things are *beliefs*? Is it really possible to believe something that is not true? Is it possible not to believe something that is true? How do you not believe something? Is not believing in something a belief?

To have knowledge, do you have to have beliefs? To have beliefs, do you have to have knowledge? What is the relationship between beliefs and knowledge?

COLOR

What is color? Can you point to an example of color? If I tell you to point to the color green, what might you point to? If we can all agree that you pointed to a green object, then it seems that we all know what sorts of things count as colors. If that is true, then can't we now say what a color is?

Is a color simply how something appears to me? Have you ever seen somebody wearing a pretty sweater or a pretty swimming suit and when people looked at it, they disagreed about whether or not it was say, green, aqua, or blue? When honest people examine the same object but continue to disagree on what color the object is, what does that suggest to you about our understanding of color?

Can a sweater really appear as a green object to one person and really appear as an aqua color to another person? Some people who are colorblind really do not see the green color in a traffic light. Does that mean that for them the color green does not exist? If the word "color" refers to a special way things appear to individual people, the green for one person may not be green to another person. Color is just the way each person sees them happen—is that correct?

What if all humans were blind, would colors exist? If all humans were blind, and if humans were always blind, do you think the word "color" would exist? If no humans existed, would colors exist? Just what exactly does the word "color" mean?

Chapter 5

EVIL

Have you ever heard people use the word "evil" before? In fairy tales a witch or sorcerer may be described as evil. What do you suppose the word "evil" means?

Imagine an older brother or sister teasing a younger brother or sister. That teasing may be described as wrong. But a simple teasing is never described as evil. Swinging a bat or tennis racquet and hitting someone accidentally may cause considerable harm. Someone may even be accused of wrongdoing or being bad for carelessly swinging the bat or racquet. But it is unlikely that anyone would accuse the wrongdoer of evil when such an accident happens. What does the word "evil" mean?

What is required for an act to truly count as an evil act? Must someone mean to do evil for a wrongful act to count as an evil act?

"Meaning to do evil" is an intention. Is that intention part of what it means to describe someone's act as an "evil" act? How does someone "mean to do evil?" How does someone "mean to do good?"

DO DINOSAURS EXIST?

Do you know what it means for something to exist? Tell me. What does it mean for something to exist? Does Snow White exist? We know that Snow White is a character in a fairy tale but does that mean she exists? Does Snow White exist outside the fairy tale?

Do the people in this room exist? How do you know the people in this room exist? Do the people in this room exist in a way that is different from the way Snow White exists in the fairy tale? What is the difference?

Do dinosaurs exist? How do you know that dinosaurs once existed? *Tyrannosaurus rex* no longer exists as a living, breathing dinosaur. What happened to the dinosaur's existence? Can something start to exist and then no longer exist?

You said above, Snow White exists in the fairy tale. Will Snow White always exist in the fairy tale? What is the difference between *Tyrannosaurus rex*'s existence and Snow White's existence?

Did *Tyrannosaurus rex* have a height, a weight, coloring, and so on? Do the people in this room each have their own height, weight, and coloring? So, height, weight, and coloring are properties that exist for people and dinosaurs. Is existence like height, weight, and coloring? Is existence a property of things that exist?

Does Snow White in the fairy tale have a weight? Does she have any properties other than existence? If existence is her only property, why say she exists?

If Snow White doesn't exist, how is it that we have been talking about her for so long and everyone seems to understand what each other is saying?

I don't understand this thing called existence. I don't even know if it should count as a property. It doesn't seem like other things we call properties. Can anyone help me understand, what is this idea we call existence?

Chapter 5
FUN

What is fun? Have each of you experienced fun before? Briefly, very briefly, give me an example of a time that was fun for you.

What makes something fun? Is fun part of an activity, perhaps playing a game or riding a bicycle? Is fun something that happens to a person when the person is doing the right thing? What is the right thing to do if you want to have fun? Can you have fun doing the wrong thing? If something is fun then, how can it be the wrong thing to do?

Plato, a Greek philosopher from nearly 2,500 years ago, explained that a person can never have fun doing the wrong thing. What do you think he meant by that?

Plato thought that a person who *thinks* he is having fun while doing the wrong thing must be mistaken about something. Plato thought that such a person was mistaken either about whether he or she was truly having fun or about whether the activity that was fun was really wrong. Plato believed that a normal person who truly understood what he or she was doing a genuinely wrongful act could not have fun while doing it. What do you think?

Fun happens to persons—not places. You may have fun in a playground, a ballpark, or at a play, but the fun you have happens *to you*, not to the place where you are having fun. What part of you has fun, your body, your brain, your mind?

Can a scientist look at you and see where the fun is happening? If I report having fun only if a particular place in my brain is also simultaneously activated, does that mean that the place of fun is that part of my brain?

What if at different times when I say I am having fun, different parts of my brain are active. Do you think that is possible? What does that tell us about where fun happens in each of us?

A heartbeat is a heartbeat no matter whose heart is beating. A brain event is a brain event no matter whose brain experiences the event. So how come some things are fun for some people and not fun for others?

What is fun? Are there different types of fun? Are some types of having fun better for you than others? Give an example of a type of fun that is generally better for people than some other type of fun. Is there any way to measure fun? If there is no way to measure fun, how do you know it exists?

If there is a way of measuring fun, should you measure each thing you might think about doing so you spend your whole life having as much fun as possible? Are some things more important than having fun? (If so, then give an example.)

Should people try to have fun? Why? Should people try to help others have fun? Why? What if helping others have fun gets in the way of your having fun, what should you do? Can it be fun helping others to have fun? Sick people can often be helped to get better by other people helping them have fun. Why do you suppose fun can have that effect on sick people? Do you think all types of fun can help sick people? Explain.

What is fun? How do you *know* when you are truly having fun? How can you *know* when someone else is having fun? Should it matter to you whether or not someone else is having fun? What should be the role of fun in your life?

Chapter 5

GOOD THINKERS

What does it mean to say that someone is smart? What does it mean to be smart? If you get good grades on tests, does that mean you are smart? If you don't get good grades on tests, does that mean you are not smart?

Does being smart mean you can remember a lot of things? What if you could remember a lot of things but you were not very good at figuring things out—could that happen to someone? I knew someone once who had a talent for remembering dates. She could tell you everyone's birthday, anniversaries, doctors' appointments, and more. However, neither she nor her friends ever thought of her as smart.

I have also known people who did not get very good grades but I thought they were smart. I think I thought they were smart because they seemed good at figuring things out. Maybe smartness combines a lot of things. Maybe to be smart you have to be good at remembering some things. Maybe to be smart you also have to be good at figuring things out. Maybe being smart is what being a good thinker is all about. What do you think about that?

How do you recognize a good thinker? What do you look for when you try to figure out if someone is a good thinker? Do good thinkers have respect for evidence? Do good thinkers respect other people's reasons that may contradict what the good thinker believes is true? Are good thinkers willing to change their mind when they recognize a flaw in their own thinking? Do good thinkers recognize the difference between something being certainly true and probably true?

How does a good thinker recognize the difference between something be true and something being only probably true? Are good thinkers quick to recognize when something that seemed true could possibly be false? How do you get good at recognizing something that appears true could possibly be false? What is a good thinker?

If you were to coach a person, that is, help a person become a better thinker, where would you start? What are the basic skills a person should develop to become a better thinker?

I once knew a person named Skye. Skye wanted to study what wood was made of. Now before we continue, remember this fact: natural wood (the kind of wood that trees are made of), has cellulose fibers that hold the tree's shape and help bring water to all its parts. Skye didn't know this fact. Skye had a tendency to just go by what she saw at the moment.

For example, in this case, she once saw her father sawing a piece of wood. Skye observed that there was sawdust all over the floor when her father sawed wood. Consequently, Skye concluded that wood was made out of sawdust. She made her decision after seeing the sawdust all over the floor where her father was sawing. What was wrong with her thinking?

Skye's friend, Hortense, told Skye that she was wrong about wood being made out of sawdust. Think about it Hortense said: "You can't scoop up a bunch of sawdust and make a tree. Of course you can make plywood and other wood products such as paper and cardboard, but those are not the natural wood of a tree." Hortense went on to explain that sawdust is what happens when you destroy wood by sawing it into parts.

Skye didn't listen to Hortense and wouldn't change her mind about wood being made out of sawdust. She just said again and again that she knows what she saw and that's all there is to it. To prove her point Skye got a saw and sawed some wood. "There," she exclaimed, "Sawdust!" His friend observed the sawdust. Then her friend said, "That doesn't prove wood is made out of sawdust. Wood and sawdust are made out of the same stuff but that doesn't make them the same things." Annoyed Skye said, "Yes it does!"

To prove her point Skye sawed more wood and then more wood and all the while the piles of sawdust got higher and more numerous. Finally, Skye said, "There's the evidence. I have proved it for you with numerous observations!"

Hortense said, "You haven't shown me anything other than what happens when you cut wood apart. Before wood is cut apart it doesn't look like or behave like a pile of sawdust. Crush an apple and you will observe some apple juice but that doesn't mean apples are made out of apple juice. Apples are made out of skin, seeds, stems juicy pulp, and so on. Your observing is OK but your thinking is all messed up."

Who is right? Who is the better thinker in this case, Skye or Hortense? Explain the reasons for your decision.

Chapter 5

KABOOM

When a tree falls in a forest does it make a sound? What is your answer to the question? Now explain why you answered the question as you did. It is funny sometimes to listen to people talk about this question. So many people rush right into answering the question but they miss an important point, namely, what does the word "sound" mean? Socrates, Plato, and Aristotle in ancient Greece would each have been quick to ask, "What do you *mean* by the word sound?" So, let's start with their question, and ask ourselves, what do we mean by the word "sound?"

I knew two people who were deaf. One was deaf because there was something wrong with the nerves in his ear. Those nerves could not send information to the brain. The other had great hearing equipment but she had a malfunction in her brain that kept the brain from using information sent to it by her ears. If both of these people were in the forest neither would report hearing the tree fall. Would they both have the *same* experience? Did one hear the sound but not know what a sound was? Did one perhaps feel a thump in the wind and yet not know that was a sound?

Perhaps *sound* has nothing to do with human *hearing*. If there were no humans in the forest, could other animals hear the sound? If there were no animals in the forest would there be a sound when a tree falls?

What does the word sound *mean*? Is a "sound" the response an animal has to certain sound *waves* passing through the air? For sound to take place must there be hearing? What if a physicist sets up a machine that can detect sound *waves* in the air? The physicist leaves after she sets up the machine. There are no animals in the forest. There is no living thing to *hear* the tree fall. The machine detects the sound waves of a falling tree. Does that mean there was a sound?

What if the machine broke just a split second before the tree falls and so the machine doesn't capture any information about waves in the air? Was there a *sound* in this case? What does the word sound mean? Could there be two definitions to the word sound? If there are two definitions to the word sound, what are they?

LUCK

Sometimes people feel like everything is going against them. Have you ever felt like that? In a country and western song there was once a line that went like this, "If it weren't for bad luck, I'd have no luck at all." Now since it was a country and western song, we won't comment on the bad grammar, using a double negative in a sentence. Instead what do you suppose the singer was trying to say when he sang, "If it weren't for bad luck, I'd have no luck at all."

What is bad luck? Have you ever had "bad luck?" How do you *know* when you have bad luck? What is good luck? Is there more good luck in the world, or more bad luck? That's a funny question, isn't it? The great philosophers of the world going back as far as Socrates, Plato, and Aristotle use to remind people that before you answer strange questions like this one about luck, you must first define your terms. If you don't define important terms, it will not be clear to anyone if the question has been answered accurately. So, let's follow the advice of the Greek philosophers now and ask: what is "luck?"

Is luck something you can have? I can have a hat, a piece of cake, a puppy. I can *have* lots of things, but is luck something a person can *have*? What does it mean to "have" something? How do you know you have something? For example, how do you know you have a hat? In what sense is having a hat like having luck? How do you know you have luck?

If you have luck, how do you know whether or not you have good luck or bad luck? Can you sometimes be mistaken about whether you have good luck or bad luck? If you can be mistaken about whether or not your luck is good or bad does that suggest luck is real? Can you show someone your good *luck*? (Notice, before you answer, I did not ask if you can show someone something good that happened to you, but I asked can you show me the luck itself.) Can you show someone your bad luck? (Again, we know bad things happen to people but that's not what we are asking to see. We are asking to see the luck itself.)

What is luck? Does luck exist? How do you know that luck exists? How do you *know* when you have luck—good or bad? Is luck a natural thing like a rock or a rose? Is luck just an imaginary idea we made up like the idea of an Easter Bunny? What is the purpose of the word "luck?"

Is luck something people create? If people create luck then we should be able to see luck itself, right? If you ask people to show you their good luck or their bad luck they usually start talking about things that happen to them. They never do get around to talking about luck. Do you think what people mean by luck is that things that just happen to them by chance?

If luck is simply whatever happens to you by chance, then it makes no sense to talk about good luck or bad luck. We can talk about the good or bad things that happen but nothing called luck causes those things—not if by luck, you mean by chance.

In biology, scientists speak of random mutations occurring by chance. They think of chance as neither a good thing, nor a bad thing . . . it is just chance. Something unpredicted occurs for seemingly no reason. It is not a matter of something being good or bad. It just is, and there seemed no way of anticipating it. It was as they say, just a chance occurrence. So, if luck is just a matter of chance, then there is no sense in speaking of good luck or, bad luck. So, why do some people talk that way? Are such people stupid or superstitious? What do you think is going on when you hear people speak of their good luck?

Is chance something you have or, something that happens to you? If luck is a matter of chance then luck happens to you and is not a matter of *having something*, right? Ok, so why do people say something like "I ran out of luck?" If you can't *have* luck, then how can you run out of it? Do you think luck is a word people use without understanding it? Do you think the word "luck" might just be a term from long ago when people were more superstitious? Is there a purpose fulfilled in people's conversation when they use the word "luck?"

Scientists talk about good luck. Usually, they use a fancy word that means the same thing. The word they use is "serendipity." By good luck (serendipity), scientists mean that something happened by chance and that they are able to make use of what happened. Bad luck, the absence of serendipity, means whatever might happen by chance was of no use. Scientists don't believe luck is something people have. To scientists, such talk about luck is just superstition or an example of how people might talk who are poorly educated. What do you think?

Is there any good use for the word luck or does it just distract us from looking for the causes of things? Do you think the Greek philosophers Socrates, Plato, and Aristotle were right about how important it is to define our terms before we begin to answer certain questions? You may have used the word "luck" quite often to talk about things that happen to you. But now, do you think you might be a little more careful about using the word? Why? What have you learned about luck? What have you learned about people who use the word luck?

Give me the most accurate definition you can imagine of the meaning of the word luck. Now, what can you say about the question we asked much earlier: is there more good luck in the world or, more bad luck? Does the question itself even make sense? It is a grammatically correct sentence? Does the sentence make sense? (Why or why not?)

Just think you learned all this by trying to get clear on the definition of the term "luck." How much more do you think you could learn if you discussed some other commonly used words in this way? So, what do you think; was it lucky we talked about this (big smile)?

PERSPECTIVE

Do you know what the word "perspective" means? People often say each person has his or her perspective on things. Have you ever seen two people get into an argument or a fight over something each person sees or hears differently? Each person may be quite honest. Each person may truly care about telling the truth. But somehow neither person can honestly agree to see or hear what the other person claims to see or hear. How do such disagreements happen?

Some people say such things happen because each person has his or her own truth. Does that make any sense? What does truth mean if each person can have his or her own truth? If each person had his or her own truth, then how could we ever successfully share ideas with each other about what is going on the world? How could we ever learn to cooperate and coordinate our collective responses to the world that is outside each of our minds?

Imagine you are sitting in a car. There is another person with you. The two of you are at an intersection where there is a stoplight. Nothing about the stoplight changes, but depending on where you are sitting, you each have your own angle on it. You each have your own perspective. Now consider again what it means to have your own perspective. Nothing in the world changes because of your unique angle in seeing the stoplight.

What changes is only your perspective. So now, in your own words, tell me what perspective is. Explain the difference between the truth and a person's perspective.

PLAY

When you go out to recess what do you do? Much of what you do at recess is play, is that right? What counts as play? When recess is over and you come back into school what happens to play?

Do you ever get into trouble in the classroom because you are playing around? I don't get it. Why would you get in trouble in school for playing around? What are you supposed to do in school?

Very famous mathematicians, economists, and physicists spend their entire lives playing with numbers. That's right "playing" with numbers. That's how they describe what they do! Some others describe what they do as their work. Can a person's work also be play? Explain.

We say that people *play* basketball. Does that mean basketball is not work? For some people can basketball be both work and play? Explain how something like basketball can be both work and play. Sometimes a parent may send a child out to play, and the child shoots baskets one after another for hours. He or she is trying to get better at shooting baskets during his or her playtime. It's his or her play time, so is he or she working or playing?

Again, can working and playing be the same thing? Describe how working and playing can be the same thing.

Is play fun? If work and play can happen together then one thing we now know is that work does not mean "*not fun!*" Work can be fun, too. Describe some work that you think is fun.

When your teacher tells you to stop playing around does she just want you to not have fun? So, why does she tell you not to play around? When you are playing around are you focused on the task at hand or are you distracted? So, when the teacher tells you to stop playing around is she telling you to stop having fun or to stop getting distracted?

Do you think teachers would like it if you had fun doing your schoolwork?

If you see work as a bad thing and play as a good thing, isn't that just your attitude? The meaning of the words "work" and "play" have nothing to do with bad or good. So, if you see work as bad and play as good that is just something you made up right?

Mathematician's work and their play is often the same thing. They play with numbers. Imagine how much you would learn if you saw everything we do in the classroom as play. Sometimes at recess or in gym, teachers may make you do something that they think is play but you don't, right? It's just no fun. But, just because it's not fun that alone doesn't make it work! Remember work can be fun.

And, for the lucky people who figure out that when work is fun, they do a better job at work than do most others. If you learn to play with numbers, ideas, adventures in stories and so on in your school, work and play both become alike, right? They are both fun.

Each time you learn something new in arithmetic, it is like learning a new rule in a game. We *play* games. Some games we play are fun, and some are not. Whether or not a game is fun depends as much on us as it does on the game oftentimes, right?

So, what makes something fun for you? What makes play fun for you? What makes work fun for you? Give an example of something you do when work and play are both the same for you. What is play?

PROBABLY/POSSIBLY

If your mother says, "We are *probably* going to have hotdogs for lunch today," what should you *expect* for lunch? Are you *sure* you will have hotdogs for lunch? Why are you *not* sure—is it because your mother used the word "probably?"

What if your mother says, "We are having hotdogs for lunch," what should you then *expect* for lunch? You might take her statement as *evidence* so you can now know you will have hotdogs for lunch. When your mother says you will probably have hotdogs for lunch. She is *being cautious* about telling you what she plans for lunch. She is telling you it is *possible* you might have something other than hotdogs for lunch.

Do you think the words "probably" and "possibly" are opposites of one another? Explain why you think that way. What about the words "always" and "never"; are they opposites of one another? Are "probably" and "possibly" more or less opposite when compared to words like "never" and "always?"

If something *never* happens or, something *always* happens, you *know* that things will never change, right? But, when someone says something *probably* happens, you know that it might *not* happen. Right? And, when someone says something may *possibly* happen you *know* that there are many chances that it might *not* happen right? Do you think that words like "probably" and "possibly" are words we use to say how much or, how little, we *know* the truth of something? Explain your thinking for us please.

When people use the words "always" and "never," they are saying something is *certainly* true right? If something is certainly true, then we can *know* it, right? If something is only probably or possibly true then *we can't say* we *know* it, can we?

The word "*always*" certainly looks like the *opposite of "never."* Each says we *know something for certain*. But, with the words "probably" or "possibly," we are *not* saying that we know anything for certain. Whatever is being talked about may or may not, happen or, may or may not be, as it seems. Does it make sense to say that words like "probably" and "possibly" are used to express *degrees of certainty* on the speaker's part? Explain how the idea of telling people degrees of certainty might work.

Is saying something is "*probably*" true similar to saying it is *kind of true*? Is saying that something could "*possibly*" be true like saying it doesn't look true but maybe could be? What does it mean to say that something could *kind of* be true? What does it mean to say that something *could possibly* be true or, *might possibly* happen?

SPACE

What is space? Can you show me where space is? If I ask you to point to a desk, you could point to an object that I can see, touch and, perhaps, smell. But what are you pointing to if you point to a space? Can I touch a space? Can I see a space? Can I smell a space?

Right now I want you to join me in looking at this desk (point to one individual desk). Is there space where this desk is sitting? If I move the desk five feet away from the place where it is sitting, will there be space at that place? How can you prove to me that there is space at that place? Does space really exist? If space really exists, then how can two different things be in exactly the same place? Let me explain what I mean.

That desk exists (point to desk), and if you say that space exists and the space and desk are two different things, then how can two different things exist at the same place? Does the space in that place only exist when the desk is not there?

If we move the desk again, will there be space in that place? If you can't touch, taste, see, hear, or smell the space, how do you know it exists? Is space the same thing as nothing? If space is the same thing as nothing, when I move from one space to another, does that mean that I am traveling from nothing to nothing?

Is space travel "nothing travel?" Why do we have the word "space?" How does the word "space" help us share ideas with one another? What sort of ideas can we share with one another by using the word "space?" How can we use the word "space" without getting confused about what is being talked about? Do you think that most people know how to use the word "space" appropriately and without getting confused?

TRUTH TELLING

What does it mean to "tell the truth?" If it is possible to tell the truth then, it must be possible to tell something that is not true, is that right? If a person deliberately tells another person something that is not true what are they telling the person? People sometimes lie or find other ways to deceive each other, right? So, a person can hide the truth or a person can reveal the truth. Is that right? What other sorts of things can be hidden?

What sort of thing is truth? Obviously, truth must be the sort of thing that can be hidden from others and it is the sort of thing that can be revealed to others. With that knowledge about truth in mind, tell me, "What sort of thing is truth?"

Now that we have some sort of idea about what truth is, can you tell me what "truth telling" is? Does "truth telling" always involve some intention? Explain. If truth telling involves an intention to be honest, does truth hiding involve an intention as well? What intention is involved when a person tries to hide the truth from others?

Long ago a lot of people thought the world was flat. If asked about the shape of the world these people would say, "It is flat." These people were not reporting the truth. On the other hand, these people were not lying. In no way were they trying to hide the truth from others. They just didn't know what the truth was.

It was something of an accident that they spoke falsely about the shape of the world. They didn't know what the truth was. They simply believed what was false to be true. When asked what their intentions were in saying the world is flat, they would presumably say, "We intend to tell the truth." So, is intention a part of truth telling? Explain. Can intention be a part of truth telling but not a part of the truth itself? Explain what you mean. Is intention a part of lying or otherwise trying to deceive others? Is it possible to lie accidentally? Explain your thinking.

Shakespeare said that a rose by any other name smells just as sweet. Shakespeare thought it was true that roses smell sweet. His intention was to tell the truth. But telling the truth isn't the same thing as knowing the truth, is it? Why not? Why does truth telling involve intention? Why does the definition of truth itself not require reference to anyone's intention?

Truth and truth telling are two separate things. What is the difference between the two? A person can sincerely be telling the truth but get things wrong, correct? Isn't this what happened when some people were telling others they thought the world was flat?

The Truth itself, however, cannot be wrong or false, can it? Wrong or false designates the opposite of truth, does it not? When truth telling a person aims at the truth, right? A person may aim at the truth but might miss the mark and not report the truth accurately. Is that right? So, what is the difference between truth telling and *the Truth* ?

Elementary Scripts

WHY "WHY" IS NOT A VERY POWERFUL QUESTION

Imagine four people. Call them Johnny von Neumann, Alan Turing, Barbara McClintock, and Maya Angelou. (In truth these are four very well-known geniuses, and so it is easy to imagine they know a lot about good questions!) Imagine each in turn got up from the table they were all sitting at, walked to the wall, and flipped the light switch. Afterward you asked each one of them, "Why did you flip the light switch?"

The mathematician von Neumann says, "Because I thought you wanted me to." The computer scientist Turing says, "Because I wanted to distract you." The poet Angelou says, "When there is an imbalance of sodium and calcium ions across cell membranes in a particular region of my corpus callosum, I move toward a light switch and flip it." The Nobel laureate in medicine McClintock says, "Because I felt like it."

Those are four very different answers to the same question. In fact, whenever you ask "why?" there is nearly always endless numbers of responses that would answer the question. So, how good is the question "why" at getting an explanation about how things are in the world?

A far more powerful question than "why" is the question: "How do you know?" In response to the question "How do you know?" not just any response will do. Ask any of the four geniuses above how they knew flipping the light switch was likely to increase or decrease the light in the room and they each have to come up with very similar answers.

They each must explain something about electricity, the workings of light bulbs and light switches. Nothing short of such an answer explains how they each could know that flipping the switch could change the lighting effect. People have to know what they are talking about to answer a "how do you know?" question.

"How do you know?" questions produce the best explanations people know how to give. So, what is the good of a "why?" question? Do "why?" questions encourage discussion? Consider which of the following two questions will encourage more discussion: "Why did you like the play *Peter Pan*?" and "How do you know the play *Peter Pan* is a classic?"

Can a lot of people freely answer the first question? Why is that? Is the second question kind of scary? To answer the question about how you know the Peter Pan play is a classic, you have to produce information that presumably most would also agree on, right? When do you think it is best to ask "why?" When do you think it is best to ask "how do you know?"

Chapter 5

WORD MEANINGS

What grade are you in? What counts as the "big kids" to you? Do you remember three years ago? Did you once think children your age were the "big kids?" Does the concept "big" change from one person to the next?

Look at your hands. Do they look big to you? Do your father's hands look big to you? What counts as "big?" Does the meaning of the word "big" change depending on who is using it, at what time the person is using the word, and under what surrounding conditions? Were your hands once much smaller than they are now? Does that mean your hands are now big when compared to then? If your hands are big now, why aren't they the same size as your father's hands? Didn't you say his hands are big?

What does the word "big" mean? Imagine two glasses are on a table. One is large and the other is small. A small child from across the street is visiting you. The small child asks you to hand her the large glass. Do you think you know which glass she is talking about?

Now, imagine your mother walks in the room, and asks you why you handed the small child such a big glass. Do you think all three of you are talking about the same glass? This makes it sound like you all understand what words like large and big mean. It sounds like there is a single meaning for such words and each of you understand the meaning of these two words. Why do you suppose that is?

Do you think the fact that there are only two glasses present serve as a clue? What else about the meaning of the words make it possible for each of the three of you to talk about the same glass?

Do different words mean different things to different people? If words mean different things to different people, how could any of us ever understand another person? If words mean different things to different people, what good would dictionaries be? Why would anyone bother to look up a word in a dictionary? Is there any reason to believe words have some common meaning that we can all share? Is there any reason to believe that that shared meaning is the reason people can share thoughts, plans, ideas, and feelings with one another?

If a word means something different to each of three or four different people, can they use that word to share an idea? Why not? In the days of ancient Greece, there were very smart people called philosophers. When philosophers began to talk with each other about anything serious, they always began by trying to define the important words they might use. Do you think that is a good idea? Why? Today philosophers, mathematicians, and physicists in particular are all very fussy about defining important terms to one another. Do you think that helps them share ideas with one another any better?

Have you ever seen some people get into an argument because one of them misunderstood a word he or she was using when talking to the other? Do you think arguments can sometimes be avoided if people are more careful to make sure they share the same meanings for important words they are using in a conversation? Do words mean different things to different people?

Chapter 6

Building Your Own Scripts

Before describing how to build a script, we will describe how Plato, history's master script builder, might describe the process. In *The Republic* Plato outlines the education he thinks is necessary in the making of philosopher kings. You need not be a philosopher king to write a script. But the preparation of a philosopher king would go far toward preparing one for writing such scripts.

According to Plato, the education of a philosopher king should initially be much like that of all other educated people. It should include physical training, the arts and sciences, geometry, and principles of social decorum. When people reach their twenties, it is then time to go out into the world and collect experience. After a dozen or more years of collecting experience, at about the age of thirty-five, the men and women are ready to begin advanced philosophical studies.

Plato believed a person needed a foundation in general learning supported by substantial real-world experience in order to learn how to advise others on living together, seeking individual purpose, and generally understanding the world at a subtle level. After fifteen years or so years of such study, the survivors of that rigorous preparation are ready to lead others forward in a collaborative and successful engagement with all that life has to offer. On this reading of Plato's preparation of philosopher kings one can imagine he had in mind a sort of extended Navy Seals boot camp for the elite intelligentsia. *We have nothing like that in mind*!

What we draw from Plato and what is applicable to building one's own scripts is that one must begin with a strong and broadly based educational background. In addition, one must become the sort of person who is very alert when collecting practical experience. A competent script builder should always be summing and revising a sense of the world in which we all live.

Philosophy is about shared understanding. When setting out to build a script the task is to tantalize and challenge students to seek better understanding and shared explanation at every turn. The task is not to say things you like or want to be true, or contriving to get others to agree with you, the script builder. The task is to pave the way toward independent and shared ventures in truth seeking for each and every discussion participant.

At the beginning of every disciplinary study there is a need for some ritualized sharing of signaling as Robin Wiley describes it in his book *Noise Matters* (2015). From learning the alphabet and how to count, to learning the periodic table, chording on pianos and banjos, and even learning to solve quadratic equations there is a need to simply be told or shown how to do something until you get it right.

But never forget that the point of learning anything is to use the acquired material to think independently and engage in the Great Conversation of Humankind. There is a threshold at which novices have learned enough to engage further material in a reflective manner. In some cases, this threshold to more reflective thinking (contrary to Plato) may begin as early as kindergarten.

Evolution crafted humans' learning instinct thousands of years ago. Consequently, scripts are aimed at enticing the natural instinct of learners to figure out why they and others think about a subject as they do. Scripts entice students to probe two questions over and again, questions that lead to an ever deeper understanding of some subject. The first question that permeates all of scripting exercises is: "How do you know?" The second question is: "What do you mean by X?" Creating a script for students requires knowing enough about the subject matter and having sufficient experience to ask questions and elicit hypotheses from students.

The script then presents counterexamples that often create cognitive dissonance and lure participants into deeper reflection. Most scripts also require a willingness to "finish" a script with an open-ended question. Consequently, do not expect scripts to end in some sort of grand T-R-U-T-H. Rather, successfully completed scripts end well when participants acquire a well-earned sense of satisfaction that they have made progress in their shared understanding of some matter. More importantly, when they truly appreciate that there may still be more to understand.

Suffice it to say that one should not take the creating of scripts lightly, no matter how easy we make it sound in the pages ahead. Take your time, and always consider revising a script after you have field tested it a few times with different classes.

PICKING A TOPIC

This may be the most important bit of advice in this chapter. When picking a topic for a script, *pick a topic that excites you.* When you are excited, the excitement is infectious. Everyone has been in a class when it was clear the instructor did not care about the topic. The instructor's lack of interest makes it difficult for students to get a feel for a subject since the subject evidently disinterests the instructor. So, your first step in picking a topic is to pick one that excites you.

Pick a topic you find intriguing and that you would be interested in learning your students' thoughts about it. Your interest and intrigue are likely to be infectious among your students. If you have ever been to a rock concert or a political convention when the star first appears, the frenzied cheering of the crowd was infectious was it not?

Of course, while the topic of a script should be exciting to you, it must also fit into the subject matter the students are studying. This does not mean that the topic must be rubric fashioned to anticipate test items students may encounter on a standardized test. It means only that you as the script builder, should use judicious discernment and select a topic that is relevant to something that the students are studying. The topic must also be one that the scripter has reasonable expectation that the students involved are generally prepared to contribute to this moment of the Great Conversation that you are designing for them.

FOCUS

Once you have a topic in mind, you must narrow your focus. To do this, single out one or two terms that represent concepts central to the subject of the script. These terms should be the object of laser-like focus in the development of your script. For example, if you want to explore the idea of *reasonableness* you might start by focusing attention of the word "reason." Thus, one can *have* a reason, one *can reason*, one can *give* a reason, and so on.

The first use of the term draws attention to how a reason plays a role in the construction of an argument or plan. The reason a student may want an "A" on the report card is to get a financial reward of some sort. In contrast, the second and third uses of the term draw attention to the idea of inferential process. One may reason when setting up an experimental apparatus and procedure for competition in a science fair. One can also reason about the wisdom of buying a lottery ticket. Finally, one can ignore reason and whimsically tell the cashier to keep a dollar in change in return for a lottery ticket.

KICK OFF

Once you have one or two terms in mind it is then time to think about how to start this moment in the Great Conversation. More often than not the way to announce this entry into the Great Conversation is by asking a question about the meaning of the key word you now have in mind. For example, if you are talking about reasonableness you might begin by simply asking the open-ended question, "What is a reason?" Isn't this the way we enter into real conversations with one another?

Each of the scripts in this book has a title. The title is solely for the purpose of helping distinguish the content of one script from another. *Never start a scripted discussion by announcing to students the title of the script.* By announcing a title you immediately move the discussion away from genuine conversation to that of another classroom exercise.

In the world outside of classrooms, people do not begin conversations by announcing a title for a topic they want to discuss. In the world outside the classroom, when a person wants to initiate a discussion he or she usually starts by asking a question. Too often, the leading question is long winded and may even contain a hint of the answer the speaker wants. This is not how to begin a scripted discussion. The leading question should be brief and open ended and give participants a chance to get their feet wet.

FOLLOW UP

Following the first question there are usually, but not always, further questions that move participants more deeply into the conversation. These follow-up questions are intended to lure students into an early consensus on how to think about the matter at hand. There may also be an early exposition of a noncontentious example. The point at this early stage is to draw the students into a false sense of security thinking that "I've got this!"

Psychologist Leon Festinger (1957) showed that when students commit to the truth and then find their truth in peril, they are generally eager to engage in discussion to relieve the cognitive dissonance. Cognitive dissonance occurs when persons feel confident they know something and yet also face sound reason denying that they know what they think they know.

This mental agitation is relieved by coming to grips with the apparent paradox, oxymoron, or whatever other mental illusion created the incoherence. Incoherence is an acknowledged mismatch between two things one believes. The script should anticipate a likely consensus students will converge toward. This initial, tentatively held, consensus gives everyone a dog in the race until confronted with an anomaly.

THE CRITICAL REVIEW

The next step in developing a script is creating grounds for critical review. Most typically this can be accomplished by creating a scenario that seems, on the surface, to run counter to the previous consensus. For example, if students generally agreed that a reason is something that causes action, the scenario offered might show how a reason may cause a change of belief in someone without causing any subsequent action. The purpose here is to create something of an "Aha" moment for students by showing them that things may not be as simple as they appear.

When this works, participants in the discussion have an additional angle (in this case on the idea of reason) that they may have never previously considered. Note that the idea that reasons are all about actions has not been discarded. Some students may persist in arguing that mental actions are like the physical actions, and they will give their most plausible reasons for maintaining their initial convictions. In contrast, students who abandon their initial convictions because of the counterexample will likely pose various hypotheses for identifying reasons more accurately, and not just as causes for action.

At this point students can be fully engaged in a critical review of the concept *reason*. Questions can be raised, such as "What do reasons do?", "What are reasons for?", "How do we know when we come across a reason?", "What is the connection between reasons and conclusions?", and "What is the role of reasons in being reasonable?" Here the script maker is posing questions in a logical sequence that slows students from jumping to conclusions. Here the scriptwriter is revealing to participants what it means to reflectively turn a thought over in one's mind—as Socrates so often encouraged.

This is the heart of the script. It is here that the script maker's talent is most prominently exhibited. Students must be engaged in a discussion that matters: seeking right answers as opposed to wrong ones, truth as opposed to falsehood, meaningfulness as opposed to nonsense, usefulness as opposed to mere fancy.

Too often discussions in classrooms degenerate into a "hide and seek" format or to a "whatever" format. In the "hide and seek" format the only point to the discussion is to get to the teacher's hidden answer. When students feel that this is going on it turns the discussion into little more than a simple game like Twenty Questions. In the "whatever" format the teacher announces at the beginning that in the discussion ahead there are no right or wrong answers! Truly? If so then, why have the discussion at all? Isn't this wasting time?

Most scripted discussions are intended to avoid identifying any position as T-R-U-T-H. But it is very important for students to realize that, while they may not be able to identify grand cosmic truth in any sense, their shared investigation can lead them away from error. When students are able to figure a way to free themselves from error the inherent value of critical review becomes evident. Every scripted discussion should embody the implicit promise that discussion may lead to better shared understanding. In the end, diversity of position may continue, but reasons for opposing positions should become transparent to all.

FINAL CONSIDERATIONS

The major steps for creating a script have now been described. However, as the saying goes, "The devil is in the details." In what follows we discuss the important details of appropriate language, of proper length, of relevant examples, of paragraphing, and of a tactic we call "sneaking in scholar's names."

Appropriate language: Keep in mind is that scripts are intended to *lead* conversations not *manage* them. The difference between leading and managing a conversation is much the same as the difference between leading and managing any human endeavor. *Leading* is a matter of getting folks to embrace their own decision-making capacities. It means getting participants to follow a discussion because it engages them in ways that matter.

In contrast, *managing* employs manipulative strategies for ensuring the discussion goes in the direction the manager intends. Managers are responsible for getting everyone to a previously dictated destination, but leaders *lead* by keeping a general shared focus before the minds of all the participants.

Managers download information and directives. The language they use is unavoidably pointed. They do not invite contributions beyond requests for clarification of what they, the manager, meant. The language of managers also has a "talking down to" quality. Managers want their audience to "get it, not share it," and certainly not to contrast novel hypotheses. Leaders keep people inspired. Leaders keep people continuously moving forward (Wagner & Simpson, 2009). When teachers use scripts the purpose is to inspire and share, not manage and direct.

Teachers can be leaders as easily as they can be managers. A teacher can sit down after school with a group of students and just talk. During these sit-down talks the teacher talks in her own voice without trying to talk down to the students. During such sit-down talks the teacher listens and questions. There is no drill and grill, no cues to recognize an answer on a quiz. *The point here is that the language used in a script should sound like a sit-down talk.* The language should capture the script maker's natural way of speaking. If during a sit-down talk the teacher uses a word students are unfamiliar with, chances are they will naturally figure it out in context.

If it is natural for the script maker to say the word "cognitive," then use it. Participants at nearly any age will figure out its meaning in context. For example, imagine nine-year-olds engaged in a script that has a sentence such as "Are reasons just *cognitive* or do you think they sometimes involve emotions too?" Nine-year-olds probably aren't familiar with the word "cognitive." But some will figure it out right away; others will figure it out by being a part of a community of peers who begin to use the word naturally with their script-using teacher. Finally, participants who haven't caught on to the meaning of the word will, in a trusting environment, ask, "What does cognitive mean?"

The bottom line is when building a script use language reflective of how you speak naturally. Sentences should *sound* right, not *read* right. A script is not an essay. It is a script meant to sustain animation throughout a conversation. Don't be afraid to use a colloquialism. Don't be afraid to use a folksy language. For example, in discussing the difference between good reasons and bad reasons you might ask: "President Obama once said, 'You can put lipstick on a pig but it is still a pig.' Does that mean that even good reasons can't make a bad idea anything other than a bad idea?" Colorful examples and analogies invigorate sit-down discussions.

Length: Scripts for younger elementary school students should always be kept short. Even though you are not dictating information to be memorized, the limited attention span of young children will make even the most cleverly constructed script a tedious task when the discussion lasts beyond thirty minutes. Scripts that create fifteen- to twenty-minute discussions are likely to be most effective with the youngest students.

As students mature, they can sustain their interest in a discussion for a longer time. However, that doesn't mean that effective scripts for older students need to be longer. What it does mean is that as students mature, scripts of varying lengths can be effectively employed. Longer scripts for older students may contain more than one counterexample or even a description of a situation contrived to set up further discussion. Keep in mind that the purpose of the script is not to impart information, but rather to enable students to use more effectively the ideas they may already have in mind.

Relevant examples: Examples in scripts are not meant to teach new material for assimilation. Scripted examples are intended to provoke cognitive dissonance or at least appreciation of the value in further review. Scripted counterexamples extend—what Vygotsky (1978, p. 78) calls the "zone of proximal development."

Scripts cause students to employ ideas they are familiar with, but in heretofore unconsidered ways. Examples should prompt students to consider new wrinkles and produce cognitive dissonance. Scripted examples must be accessible to students' range of experience and imagination. Try to draw upon well-entrenched experiences of the students as often as possible.

The more mature the students, the more novel or extensive may be the presentation of new information, or the introduction of an extended scenario. Less mature students need information delivered with optimal brevity.

Less mature students need to see issues more transparently displayed in the unfolding of a scenario or a series of questions. Less mature students also need to be primed with truncated scenarios that prompt discussion or an inviting question in sixty to ninety seconds or less.

If characters are named in the scenario try to use proper names that sound familiar to students in the locale wherein your scripts are to be used. Again, the reason is to make entry into the discussion as inviting as possible. The discussion should have the feel of a familiar event, an interesting chat students might have with a slightly more worldly and sophisticated friend. Names that sound exotic, just as scenarios that seem too far-fetched given the experience of the less mature students, become distracting and an impediment to their readily engaging in the discussion.

THE PRINCIPLE OF FAMILIARITY
AND SNEAKING IN NAMES OF SCHOLARS

We have already made clear that language, additional information, and scenarios should adhere to a *Principle of Familiarity*. The principle of familiarity states simply that scripted discussions should begin well within participants' collective zone of proximal development.

There is a difference between *knowing that* and *knowing how*. For example, we *know that* there are four authors of this book. Knowing that fact tells the reader nothing about *knowing how* to read this book in order to extract from it as much meaning as possible. This book is about developing further *know how* in students. It is not a book-cataloging fact for drill and grill. This means that adhering to the Principle of Familiarity is critical for ensuring that students feel welcomed into participation rather than challenged to grasp new facts as a result of scripted discussion.

Nonetheless, will the students learn new facts and ideas despite that not being an objective of the script? Ask them. If the script was successfully constructed, when you ask students if they learned from their participation in the scripted discussion you will learn three things.

First, you will learn that the students believe they learned a great deal about their own thinking on the topic. Second, students will report that they learned the ideas discussed were much more involved than they initially expected. Third, they will report that they learned important things from one another and not just from the script maker downloading information. When students report awareness of their learning these things, you will have confirmation that you brought the students into a moment of the Great Conversation of Humankind.

Paying attention to the Principle of Familiarity does not preclude using some language that may be unfamiliar to students. Sometimes the script maker may so love a certain author that the script maker wants to build the author's name into a script. This is perfectly all right—on occasion. However, the scripter must not be tempted to test students over the name of a person mentioned in a script. To test students on the script in this fashion will cause the script to deteriorate into nothing other than an exercise in Piagetian assimilation.

For example, in writing this book we, the authors, find ourselves drawn to share with the reader that, while many writers have made allusion to the distinction between knowing how and knowing that, the first one to do so using those exact words, was legendary philosopher Gilbert Ryle (2000). Sometimes such attributions are done to give credit where credit is due—especially in scholarly journals. At other times such attributions may turn out to be little more than a bit of hero worship. Such hero worship is fine unless it becomes an object of subsequent examination. Knowing about Gilbert Ryle makes no student a higher-level thinker.

If the student picks up a passing acquaintance with the name of a famous intellect and that happens to lead to further biographical interest in that person, great. But such learning is incidental to the process scripts focus on. The incidental learning should never distract from the core process. Slipping in a name or two is a luxury for the script builder. It is a luxury because the focus of the exercise is to develop students' higher-level thinking skills and not simply to add to memorized data to be assimilated. Slipping in a name primarily provides the script builder the satisfaction of knowing students have at least heard the name of some favored intellect.

There is one other reason for slipping in a name. If the script builder is crafting a script for a particular lesson, bringing in a name the students are familiar with may provide some contextual familiarity. A script developed for a particular subject may also be a way to introduce a figure central to some future curriculum without making it a centerpiece of didactic instruction. A history teacher, for example, may find using the name Aristotle beneficial in context, or a science teacher might find Mendeleev worth mentioning prior to instruction involving the periodic table.

THE SCRIPT YOU BUILD WILL BE YOUR OWN

When building your script subordinate your personal whims and convictions to the creative robustness of the script. There is an upside and a downside to this rather obvious directive. The upside is that when building a script you are investing in a discussion you excitedly anticipate sharing with students. The downside is that it is very difficult not to sell your ideas, leveraging your authority as scripter to ensure a consensus you favor. Inoculate students against any unintentional indoctrination on your part by simply reminding yourself again and again that your task is to *lead participants into a discussion.*

Leading students into a discussion means that you must exercise the courage and trust your students to follow their own path when achieving higher-level thinking skills is the goal. Students learning just what you know is not students doing higher-level thinking. Instead, students figuring out matters, working together in a quest of truth seeking and shared understanding constitute the intellectual challenge of the Great Conversation and this is what scripted discussions are all about.

Resources for Further Information
An Annotated List

WEBSITE AT SAM HOUSTON STATE UNIVERSITY

You now have a good start developing critical thinking in your students as your mandated curriculum may allow. Your supply of scripts may well fill up a year. Then again, maybe not. In case you have a need for further scripts, we outlined the protocol for writing your own scripts.

Some teachers may not want to write their own scripts or they may be unsure if a script they are writing models the scripts contained herein sufficiently to be effective. Rather than abandon you to make it or break it on your own, we intend to stand by and assist you as much as we can and as much as you may wish. To do this, we have established a website at Sam Houston State University (SHSU) to continue to assist you as your time and needs evolve.

The website will serve several purposes. First, you may submit questions about script content, discussion structure, or request review of a script you have prepared on your own. You can expect a return from us in four business days while school is in session each year. Second, from time to time we post a new script on the website that will be freely available to all users of the system.

Third, if schools or districts decide they would like a workshop or even a year-long piloted program in their district, they can contact the website to request one or more of the authors to respond and manage the request in detail. Finally, there are a number of programs around the world that develop communities of inquiry for students in one way or another. The website will maintain a clearinghouse of such programs to the extent that we know about them. The address of the website is http://thinkingbeyondthetest.weebly.com. For additional information, the phone number to contact Daphne Johnson at Sam Houston is (936) 294-3875.

BOOKS ON ENGAGING STUDENTS IN COMMUNITIES OF INQUIRY

A. *Thinking Through Philosophy* books 1, 2, 3, and 4 (2002) by Paul Cleghorn and Stephanie Baudet. Each book in the series features a number of stories, mysteries, and other discussion starters and a step-by-step process for creating and maintaining a community of inquiry in the classroom. Book 4 in particular provides the teaching materials for the study reported in Fair et al. (2015a) and for the earlier study reported by Topping and Trickey (2007a). The books in the series are available for downloading for about $25 each from Educational Printing Services Ltd.
B. *Argue With Me* (second edition, 2016) by Deanna Kuhn, Laura Hemberger, and Valerie Khait is available from Routledge. This book is based on Deanna Kuhn's highly regarded, decades-long research study of argumentation skills, and it is a handbook intended to aid the classroom teacher in developing her students' skills at argumentation and, subsequently, their writing skills.
C. *The Philosophical Child* (2012) by Jana Mohr Lone and *Philosophy in Education* (2016) by Jana Mohr Lone and Michael D. Burroughs. Both books are available from Rowman & Littlefield. The earlier book gives an introduction to structuring dialogues in the classroom on open-ended topics, while the second mostly furnishes a set of materials for classroom use.
D. *Big Ideas for Little Kids* (2009) by Thomas Wartenberg is also available from Rowman & Littlefield. It uses children's literature, for example, *The Giving Tree*, to lead students into discussing philosophical ideas.
E. Finally, an older book from Temple University Press, *Philosophy in the Classroom* (1980, second edition) by Matthew Lipman, Ann Margaret Sharp, and Frederick Oscanyan, gives the interested reader an overview of topics such as "Encouraging Children to Be Thoughtful" and "Applying Thinking Skills to School Experience."

INSTITUTIONS THAT SUPPORT PROGRAMS TO INVOLVE STUDENTS IN THE GREAT CONVERSATION

A. The University of Hawai'i at Manoa Uehiro Academy for Philosophy and Education at http://p4chawaii.org. This program has been ongoing for a number of years and you can find all sorts of resources from a link on their homepage. One of the important things this program stresses is how structured discussions of serious questions in the school classroom contribute to cross-cultural understanding. Here is a portion of their operating philosophy: "Schools must move from being institutions that provide students with extrinsic meanings to institutions that provide students with the necessary circumstances and tools that will allow each to personally construct meaning in their own learning and lives."

B. Under the direction of the founder, Jana Mohr Lone, the University of Washington's Center for Philosophy for Children was begun in 1996 and is now affiliated with the University of Washington's Philosophy Department. The center's website is at http://depts.washington.edu/nwcenter/aboutintroduction.html. It gives one access to a great deal of useful information, for example, a video of a classroom discussion https://www.youtube.com/watch?v=KfxgjFyBnAQ. The site also includes a set of model lesson plans and links to a number of helpful websites, including, for example, a program at the University of Texas El Paso, Philosophy for Children in the Borderlands.

C. In 1974, at Montclair State University the Institute for the Advancement of Philosophy for Children (IAPC) was founded with Matthew Lipman as the leading light. Since that time, the IAPC has published a number of books relating to Philosophy for Children (P4C), sponsored conferences, journals, and research on P4C. For information on current activities, including an IAPC Summer Seminar contact Joe Oyler at oylerj@mail.montclair.edu and visit the website http://www.montclair.edu/cehs/academics/centers-and-institutes/iapc/

D. SAPERE is a British group that supports P4C, and their website at http://www.sapere.org.uk gives anyone interested a chance to see what this can look like in the classroom. Also, SAPERE partnered with the Education Endowment Foundation to sponsor a major study of how dialogues on concepts such "truth" and "fairness" could affect the achievement levels of students in years four and five. According to the Durham University group who evaluated the study, the program had a positive impact on students' reading and math, and this effect was biggest on disadvantaged students. See the report: https://v1.educationendowmentfoundation.org.uk/uploads/pdf/Philosophy_for_Children.pdf. Finally, for a number of video clips that show P4C in action in school classrooms see http://www.sapere.org.uk/default.aspx?tabid=189.

RESOURCES FOR CRITICAL THINKING THEORY, PEDAGOGY, AND PRACTICE

A. There are a number of textbooks that convey an overall sense of what can be involved in the effort to teach critical thinking principles and practices. A couple of the standard texts are *Critical Thinking: Consider the Verdict* by Bruce Waller (sixth edition, 2012) and *The Power of Critical Thinking* by Lewis Vaughn (fifth edition, 2015). Two innovative books in this area are *Reason in the Balance* by Sharon Bailin and Mark Battersby (second edition, 2016) and *THINK Critically* by Peter Facione and Carol Gittens (second edition, 2013).

B. In addition to Daniel Kahneman's book *Thinking, Fast and Slow*, there are several books by psychologists that should be of interest to anyone concerned with critical thinking, books such as *Mindware: Tools for Smart Thinking* by Richard Nisbett (2015), *What Intelligence Tests Miss: The Psychology of Rational Thought* by Keith Stanovich (2010), and the classic *How We Know What Isn't So* by Tom Gilovich. See *Risk Savvy: How to Make Good Decisions* (2014) by Gerd Gigerenzer for a somewhat contrarian view.

C. There are several websites that offer a variety of "takes" on what critical thinking involves. One is Insight Assessment, which is a source for some of the most widely used tests to assess critical thinking skills and dispositions (http://www.insightassessment.com). Another website that features materials inspired by the work of Richard Paul is http://www.criticalthinking.org//. For a sample of this approach to critical thinking, a handy source is *Learning to Think Things Through: A Guide to Critical Thinking Across the Curriculum* by Gerald Nosich (fourth edition, 2011). Here is a website that is off the beaten track somewhat, but it offers an approach to critical thinking as involving dialogue as an essential component: http://www.cog-tech.com.

D. Here are some useful journals:
   1. *Inquiry: Critical Thinking Across the Disciplines*, Sam Houston State University, three issues (print and online versions)

   Inquiry: Critical Thinking Across the Disciplines is a forum for the discussion of issues related to the theory, practice, and pedagogy of critical thinking across the disciplines, from precollege to university settings. The goal is to encourage an exchange of ideas about effective pedagogy in critical thinking instruction, about methods of assessing critical thinking skills and dispositions, about systematic errors in our thinking, about enhancing the quality of information on which we base decisions and inferences, about common fallacies in argumentation, and about all other topics that are relevant to critical thinking across the disciplines.

   2. *Informal Logic*, University of Windsor, Canada, quarterly (online version)

   Informal Logic is a peer-reviewed journal publishing articles and reviews on topics related to reasoning and argumentation in theory and

practice. It is deliberately multidisciplinary, welcoming theoretical and empirical research from any pertinent field, including, but not restricted to, philosophy, rhetoric, communication, linguistics, psychology, artificial intelligence, education, and law.

3. *Thinking and Reasoning*, Routledge, quarterly (print and online versions)

   Thinking & Reasoning is dedicated to the understanding of human thought processes, with particular emphasis on studies on reasoning, decision-making, and problem solving. While the primary focus is on psychological studies of thinking, contributions are welcome from philosophers, artificial intelligence researchers, and other cognitive scientists whose work bears upon the central concerns of the journal. Topics published in the journal fall under the broad umbrella described above and include studies of deductive reasoning, inductive reasoning, judgments of probability and other quantities, conceptual thinking, the neuropsychology of reasoning, and the influence of language and culture on thought.

4. *Thinking Skills and Creativity*, Elsevier, quarterly (print and online versions)

   Thinking Skills and Creativity is a journal providing a peer-reviewed forum for communication and debate for the community of researchers interested in teaching for thinking and creativity. Papers may represent a variety of theoretical perspectives and methodological approaches and may relate to any age level in a diversity of settings: formal and informal, education and work based.

References

Alliance for Excellent Education. (2011). *A time for deeper learning: Preparing students for a changing world.* Retrieved from http://all4ed.org/wp-content/uploads/2013/06/DeeperLearning.pdf.

Anderson, L.W., & Krathwohl, D.R. (2001). *A taxonomy for learning, teaching, and assessing: A revision of Bloom's taxonomy of educational objectives.* New York, NY: Longman.

Arrow, K. (1992). I know a hawk from a handsaw. In M. Szenberg (Ed.), *Eminent economists: Their life philosophies.* Cambridge: Cambridge University Press.

Balter, M. (1998, November). Why settle down? The mystery of communities. *Science, 20,* 1442–1446.

Bandura, A., & Walters, R. (1963). *Social learning and personality development.* New York: Holt, Rinehart and Winston.

Baron, J. (1985). *Rationality and intelligence.* Cambridge: Cambridge University Press.

Baron, J. (2007). *Thinking and deciding.* Fourth edn., New York, NY: Cambridge University Press.

Bartlett, F.C. (1950). Programme for experiments on thinking. *Quarterly Journal of Experimental Psychology, 2,* 145–152.

Benderson, A. (Ed.), (1990). *Critical thinking: Critical issues.* Princeton, NJ: Educational Testing Service.

Binmore, K. (2009). *Rational decisions.* Princeton, NJ: Princeton University Press.

Bloch, J., & Spataro, S.E. (2014). Cultivating critical-thinking dispositions throughout the business curriculum. *Business and Professional Communication Quarterly, 77,* 249–265.

Bloom, B.S., Englehart, M.D., Furst, E.J., Hill, W.H., & Krathwohl, D.R. (1956). *Taxonomy of educational objectives. Handbook 1: Cognitive domain.* New York, NY: Longman, Green.

Bowell, T., & Kemp, G. (2014). *Critical thinking: A concise guide.* Fourth ed. Florence, KY: Routledge

Bowers, J.S. (2002). Challenging the widespread assumption that connectionism and distributed representations go hand-in-hand. *Cognitive Psychology, 45*, 413–445.

Brophy, J., & Good, T. (1974) *Teacher-student relationships: Causes and consequences*. New York: Holt, Rinehart, & Winston.

Bruner, J.S. (1961). Individual and collective problems in the study of thinking. *Annals of the New York Academy of Sciences, 91*(1), 22–37.

Bruner, J.S. (1973). *The relevance of education*. New York, NY: Norton.

Bruner, J.S., Goodnow, J.J., & Austin, G.A. (1956). *A study of thinking*. New York, NY: Wiley.

Carey, N. (2015). *DNA: A journey through the dark matter of the genome*. New York, NY: Columbia University Press.

Carlgren, T. (2013). Communication, critical thinking, problem solving: A suggested course for all high school students in the 21st century. *Springer Science + Business Media, 44*, 63–81.

Chomsky, N. (1959). Review of Skinner's *Verbal Behavior. Language, 35,* 26–58.

Cohen, M.S., Adelman, L., Bresnick, T., Marvin, F.F., Salas, E., Riedel, S. L. (2006). Dialogue as medium (and message) for training critical thinking. In R. Hoffman (Ed.), *Expertise out of context* (pp. 219–262). Mahwah, NJ: Erlbaum. See also Cohen at Cognitive Technologies, Inc., at http://www.cog-tech.com.

Curry, A. (2008, January). Seeking the roots of ritual. *Science, 319*, 278–280.

Dellarosa, D. (1988). A history of thinking. In R.J. Sternberg & E.E. Smith (Eds.). *The psychology of human thought* (pp. 1–18). New York, NY: Cambridge University Press.

Dominowski, R.L., & Bourne, L.E. (1994). History of research on thinking and problem solving. In R.J. Sternberg & E.E. Smith (Eds.). *Thinking and problem solving* (pp. 1–35). New York, NY: Academic.

Ennis, R. (2011a). Critical thinking: Reflection and perspective Part I. *Inquiry: Critical Thinking Across the Disciplines, 26* (1), 4–18.

Ennis, R. (2011b). Critical thinking: Reflection and perspective Part II. *Inquiry: Critical Thinking Across the Disciplines, 26*(2), 5–20.

Ericsson, K.A., & Hastie, R. (1994). Contemporary approaches to the study of thinking and problem solving. In R.J. Sternberg & E.E. Smith (Eds.). *Thinking and problem solving* (pp. 37–79). New York, NY: Academic.

Evans, J. St. B.T. (1995). Editorial. *Thinking and Reasoning. 1*, 1–4.

Facione, P. (1990). Critical thinking: A statement of expert consensus for purposes of educational assessment and instruction. *The Delphi Report*. The California Academic Press. (See also http://www.insightassessment.com.)

Facione, P., & Gittens, C. (2012). *THINK Critically*. Second edn. Old Tappan, NJ: Pearson.

Facione, P., & Facione, N. (2013). Critical thinking for life: Valuing, measuring, and training critical thinking in all its forms. *Inquiry: Critical Thinking Across the Disciplines, 8*(1), 5–25.

Fair, F., Haas, L., Gardosik, C., Johnson, D., Price, D., & Leipnik, O. (2015a). Socrates in the schools from Scotland to Texas: Replicating a study on the effects of a Philosophy for Children program. *Journal of Philosophy in School, 2*(1), 18–27.

Fair, F., Haas, L., Gardosik, C., Johnson, D., Price, D., & Leipnik, O. (2015b). Socrates in the schools: Gains at a three-year follow-up. *Journal of Philosophy in Schools, 28*(2), 5–16.

Fasko, D. (Ed.). (2003). *Critical thinking and reasoning: Current research, theory, and practice.* Creskill, NJ: Hampton.

Festinger, L. (1957). *A theory of cognitive dissonance.* Stanford, CA: Stanford University Press.

Flynn, J. (2016). *Does your family make you smarter?* Cambridge: Cambridge University.

Frisbee, S.M., & Reynolds, S. (2014, September–October). Critical thinking: A missing ingredient in DoD's acquisition (Education) system. *Defense AT&L,* 17–21.

Gardner, H. (1983). *Frames of mind: The theory of multiple intelligences.* New York: Basic Books.

Gardner, H. (1990). Forward. In Howard, V. (Ed.), *Varieties of thinking* (pp. i–xiii). New York, NY: Routledge.

Gelernter, D. (2016). *The tides of mind.* New York, NY. Liveright.

Gigerenzer, G. (2008). *Rationality for mortals.* Oxford: Oxford University Press.

Gigerenzer, G. (2009). *Gut feelings: The intelligence of the unconscious.* New York, NY: Penguin.

Gigerenzer, G. (2014). *Risk savvy.* New York, NY: Viking Press.

Gilhooly, K.J. (1996). *Thinking: Directed, undirected, and creative.* London, England: Academic.

Gilovich, T., & Ross. L. (2015). *The wisest one in the room.* New York, NY: Free Press.

Gopnik, A. (2010). *The Philosophical baby: What children can tell us about truth, love and the meaning of life.* New York, NY: Farrar, Strauss, & Giroux.

Gredler, M.E. (2009). Hiding in plain sight: The stages of mastery/self-regulation in Vygotsky's cultural-historical theory. *Educational Psychologist, 44,* 1–19.

Gredler, M.E. (2012). Understanding Vygotsky for the classroom: Is it too late? *Educational Psychology Review, 24,* 113–131.

Grigorenko, E.L., & Sternberg, R.J. (1993). *Set of thinking styles tasks for students.* Unpublished test.

Grossberg, S. (1999). The link between brain learning, attention, and consciousness. *Consciousness and Cognition, 8,* 1–44.

Hacking, I. (1990). *The taming of chance.* New York, NY: Cambridge University Press.

Hart Research Associates (2013). *It takes more than a major: Employer priorities for college learning and student success.* Washington, DC: The Association of American Colleges and Universities.

Henrich, J. (2015). *The secret of our success.* Princeton, NJ: Princeton University Press.

Huitt, W. (2011). Bloom et al.'s taxonomy of the cognitive domain. *Educational Psychology Interactive.* Valdosta, GA: Valdosta State University. Retrieved December 28, 2015 from http://www.edpsycinteractive.org/topics/cognition/bloom.html.pdf

Inhelder, B., & Piaget, J. (1958). *The growth of logical thinking from childhood to adolescence.* New York, NY: Basic Books.

Kagan, J. (2016). *On being human: Why mind matters.* New Haven, CT: Yale University.
Kahneman, D. (2011). *Thinking, fast and slow.* New York, NY: Farrar, Straus, & Giroux.
Kahnemann, D., & Tversky, A. (1982). *Judgement under uncertainty: Heuristics and biases.* Cambridge, England: Cambridge University Press.
Kamenetz, A. (2015). *The test: Why our schools are obsessed with standardized testing - but you don't have to be.* New York, NY: Public Affairs.
Kettler, T. (2014). Critical thinking skills among elementary school students: Comparing identified gifted and general education student performance. *Gifted Child Quarterly, 58,* 127–136.
Kohn, A., (2015). *Schooling beyond measure.* Portsmouth, NH: Heinemann.
Kuhn, D. (2015). Thinking together and alone. *Educational Researcher, 44*(1), 46–53.
Langford, P.E. (2005). *Vygotsky's developmental and educational psychology.* New York, NY: Psychology Press.
Lipman, M. (1985). Thinking skills facilitated by Philosophy for Children. In J.W. Segal, S.F. Chipman, & R. Glaser (Eds.), *Thinking and learning skills* (Vol.1): Relating instruction in research (pp. 83–108). Hillsdale, NJ: Erlbaum.
Lipman, M. (2003). *Thinking in education.* New York, NY: Cambridge University Press.
Mann, C.C. (2011, June). The birth of religion. *National Geographic, 125*(2), 34–59.
Martin, D.S. (1994). Critical comparisons of thinking skills programs: Making curriculum decisions. *Inquiry: Critical Thinking Across the Disciplines, 14*(2), 11–16.
Martin, L.M., & Halpern, D.F. (2011). Pedagogy for developing critical thinking in adolescents: Explicit instruction produces greatest gains. *Thinking and Creativity, 6,* 1–13.
McCollister, K., & Sayler, M. (2010). Lift the ceiling: Increase rigor with critical thinking skills. *Gifted Child Today,* 33(1), 41–47.
McLeod, P., Plunkett, K., & Rolls, E.T. (1998). *Introduction to connectionist modeling of cognitive processes.* New York, NY: Oxford University Press.
Mlodinow, L. (2015). *The upright thinkers.* New York, NY: Pantheon.
Murphy, P., Rowe, M., Ramani, G., & Silverman, R. (2014). Promoting critical-analytic thinking in children and adolescents at home and in school. *Springer Science + Business Media, 26,* 561–578.
Murray, B. (1997). Teaching today's pupils to think critically. *APA Monitor, 28*(3), 51.
Newall, A., Shaw, J.C., & Simon, H.A. (1958). Elements of a theory of human problem solving. *Psychological Review, 65,* 151–166.
Nisbett, R. (2015). *Mindware: Tools for smart thinking.* New York: Farrar, Straus and Giroux.
Nitzan, S. (2010). *Collective preferences and choice.* Cambridge: Cambridge University Press.
Noddings, N. (1968). *Educating for intelligent belief or unbelief.* New York, NY: Teachers College Press.
Nowak, M., & Highfield, R. (2012) *Supercooperators.* New York, NY: The Free Press.
Nowak, M., Sasaki, C., & Fudenberg, D. (2004). Emergence of cooperation and evolutionary stability in finite populations. *Nature, 428,* 646–650.

Numendal, S.G., & Halpern, D.F. (1995). Introduction: Making the case for "Psychologists teach critical thinking." *Teaching of Psychology, 22*, 4–5.

Ormrod, J.E. (2015). *Essentials of educational psychology: Big ideas to guide effective teaching.* Boston, MA: Pearson.

Pascal, B. (1671/1995). *The Pensees* (A.J. Krailsheimer, Trans.). New York, NY: Penguin.

Paul, R.W. (1985). The critical thinking movement. *National Forum, 65*(1), 2–3, 32.

Paul, R.W. (1992). Critical thinking. In C.A. Barnes (Ed.), *Critical thinking: Educational imperative* (pp. 3–24). San Francisco, CA: Jossey-Bass.

Paul, R. (2011). Reflections on the nature of critical thinking, its history, politics, and barriers and on its status across the college/university curriculum Part I. *Inquiry: Critical Thinking Across the Disciplines, 26*(3), 5–24.

Paul, R. (2012). Reflections on the nature of critical thinking, its history, politics, and barriers and on its status across the college/university curriculum Part II. *Inquiry: Critical Thinking Across the Disciplines, 27*(1), 5–30.

Paul, R., & Elder, L. (2011). *Critical thinking: Tools for taking charge of your learning and your life.* Third edn. Upper Saddle River, NJ: Prentice-Hall.

Peirce, C.S. (1878) How to make our ideas clear. *Popular Science Monthly* 12 (January 1878), 286–302. It may be retrieved at http://www.peirce.org/writings/p119.html

Perkins, D. (2012) Mindware and the metacurriculum. From New Horizons for Learning, the Johns Hopkins School of Education, at http://education.jhu.edu/PD/newhorizons/future/creating_the_future/crfut_perkins.cfm

Perkins, D., Jay, E., & Tishman, S. (1993). New conceptions of thinking: From ontology to education. *Educational Psychologist, 28*, 67–85.

Petrie, H. (2011). *The dilemma of enquiry and learning.* Hayward, CA: Living Control Systems.

Pfaff, D. (2015). *The altruistic brain.* Oxford, England: Oxford University Press.

Pinker, S. (1994). *The language instinct: How the mind creates the gift of language.* New York, NY: William Morrow.

Pinker, S. (1997). *How the mind works.* New York, NY: Norton.

Rachelin, H. (1989). *Judgement, decision and choice.* New York, NY: Freeman.

Rakow, S. (1986). *Teaching science as inquiry.* Bloomington, IN: Phi Delta Kappa Educational Foundation Fastback 246.

Ravitch, D. (2009). *The death and life of the great American school system.* New York, NY: Basic Books.

Reeves, A.R. (2011). *Where great teaching begins: Planning for student thinking and learning.* Alexandria, VA: Association for Supervision and Curriculum Development.

Reid, J.R., & Anderson, P.R. (2012). Critical Thinking in the business classroom. *Journal of Education for Business, 87*, 52–59.

Ridley, M. (2015). *Evolution of everything.* New York, NY: Harper.

Rosenthal, E.C. (2014). The complete idiot's guide to game theory. Alpha Publishing.

Rummelhart, D.E., Smolensky, P., McClelland, J.L., & Hinton, G.E. (1986). Schemata and sequential thought processes in PDP models. In. J.L. McClelland, D.E. Rummelhart, & the PDP Research Group (Eds.), *Parallel distributed processing, 2*, pp. 7–57. Cambridge, MA: MIT Press.

Sachs, J. (2011). *The price of civilization: Reawakening American virtue and prosperity.* New York, NY: Random House.

Salsburg, D. (2001). *The lady tasting tea: How statistics revolutionized science in the twentieth century.* New York, NY: Freeman.

Scheffler, I. (1997). In praise of cognitive emotions. *Teachers College Record, 79*(2), 171–186.

Siegler, R.S. (1991). *Children's thinking.* Second edn. Englewood Cliffs, NJ: Prentice-Hall.

Sigel, E.E. (1984). A constructivist perspective for teaching thinking. *Educational Leadership, 42*(3), 18–21.

Sigmund, K., Hauert, C., & Nowak, M. (2001). Reward and punishment. *Proceedings of the national academy of sciences of the USA, 98,* 10757–10762.

Simon, H. (1982). *Models of bounded rationality.* Cambridge, MA: MIT Press.

Sosa, E. (2009). *A virtue epistemology: Apt belief and reflective knowledge, Volume I.* Oxford, England: Clarendon.

Stanovich, K.E. (2009). Rational and irrational thought: The thinking that IQ tests miss. *Scientific American Mind, 20*(6), 34–39.

Stanovich, K.E., & West, R.F. (1997). Reasoning independently of prior belief and individual differences in actively open-minded thinking. *Journal of Educational Psychology, 89,* 342–357.

Sternberg, E.J. (2016). *Neurologic.* New York, NY: Pantheon.

Sternberg, R.J. (1994). Thinking styles: Theory and assessment at the interface between intelligence and personality. In R.J. Sternberg & P. Ruzgis (Eds.), *Intelligence and personality* (pp. 169–187). New York, NY: Cambridge University Press.

Sternberg. R.J. (1997a). Styles of thinking and learning. *Canadian Journal of School Psychology, 13,* 15–40.

Sternberg, R.J. (1997b). *Thinking styles.* New York, NY: Cambridge University Press.

Sternberg, R.J. (2003). Styles of thinking. In D. Fasko (Ed.). *Critical thinking and reasoning: Current research, theory, and practice* (pp. 67–87). Cresskill, NJ: Hampton.

Sternberg, R.J., & Grigorenko, E.L. (1995). Styles of thinking in the school. *European Journal of High Ability. 6,* 201–219.

Sternberg, R.J., & Grigorenko, E.L. (1997). Are cognitive styles still in style? *American Psychologist, 52,* 700–712.

Sternberg, R.J., & Wagner, R.K. (1991). *MSG thinking styles inventory manual.* Unpublished test manual.

Sternberg, R.J., & Zhang, Li-fang. (2005). Styles of thinking as a basis of differentiated instruction. *Theory into Practice, 44,* 245–253.

Syed, M. (2016). *Black box thinking.* New York, NY: Penguin.

Taleb, N. (2007). *The black swan.* New York, NY: Random House.

Taleb, N. (2014). *Antifragile.* New York, NY: Random House.

Taylor, J. (2009). *Not a chimp.* New York, NY: Oxford University Press.

Thaler, R. (2015). *The making of behavioral economics.* New York, NY: Norton.

Tomasello, M., (2014). *A natural history of human thinking.* Cambridge, MA: Harvard University Press.

Topping, K., & Trickey, S. (2007a). Collaborative philosophical enquiry for school children: Cognitive effects at 10–12 years. *British Journal of Educational Psychology, 77*, 271–288.

Topping, K., & Trickey, S. (2007b). Collaborative philosophical inquiry for schoolchildren: Cognitive gains at 2-year follow-up. *British Journal of Educational Psychology, 77*, 787–796.

Torff, B. (2005). Developmental changes in teachers' beliefs about critical-thinking activities. *Journal of Educational Psychology, 97*, 13–22.

Tversky, A., & Kahneman, D. (1974). Judgment under uncertainty: Heuristics and biases. *Science, 185*, 1124–1131.

Wagner, P.A. (1990). Will education contain fewer surprises in the future? In V. Gardner (Ed.), *Varieties of thinking* (pp. 142–173). New York, NY: Routledge.

Wagner, P.A. (2011). Socio-sexual education: A practical study in formal thinking and teachable moments. *Sex Education, 11*(2), 193–211.

Wagner, P.A. (2013). Game theory and psychological investigation. In H. Hannapi (Ed.), *Game theory unlaunched* (pp. 325–344). Rijeka, Croatia: Intech.

Wagner, P.A. & Lopez, G. (2013). The great conversation of humankind and the ethics of inclusion. *Multicultural Perspectives, 12*(3), 167–172.

Wagner, P.A., & Simpson, D. (2009). *Ethical decision-making in educational administration*. San Francisco, CA: Sage.

Weisdorf, J.L. (2005). From foraging to farming: Explaining the Neolithic revolution. *Journal of Economic Surveys, 19*, 562–586.

Weissberg, R. (2013). Critically thinking about critical thinking. *Springer Science + Business Media, 26*, 317–328.

Wiley, R. (2015). *Why noise matters*. Cambridge, MA: Harvard University Press.

Yeh, S. (2002). Tests worth teaching to: Constructing state-mandated tests that emphasize critical thinking. *Educational Researcher, 30*(9), 12–17.

Author Index

Alliance for Excellent Education, 4
Anderson, L.W., 30, 31

Bandura, A., 11
Baron, J., 24, 25, 33
Bartlett, F.C., 29
Binmore, K., 17
Bloch, J., 3
Bloom, B.S., 30, 31
Bourne, L.E., 27
Bowers, J.S., 32
Brophy, J., 47
Bruner, J.S., 32

Chomsky, N., 29
Cohen, M. S., 10

Dellarosa, D., 27, 28, 31
Dominowski, R.L., 27

Elder, L., 5, 10
Englehart, M.D., 30
Ennis, R., 8
Ericsson, K.A., 33
Evans, J., 28

Facione, P., 9, 90
Fair, F., 10, 48, 88
Fasko, D., 6, 35

Festinger, L., 46, 80
Flynn, J., 8
Frisbee, S.M., 3
Furst, E.J., 30

Gardner, H., 11, 33
Gigerenzer, G., 4, 10, 21, 24, 25
Gilhooly, K.J., 27, 32
Gittens, C., 90
Good, T., 47
Gopnik, A., 44
Gredler, M.E., 28
Grigorenko, E.L., 35
Grossberg, S., 32

Hacking, I., 24
Hastie, R., 33
Henrich, J., 44
Highfield, R., 41
Hill, W.H., 30
Hinton, G.E., 32
Huitt, W., 31

Inhelder, B., 30

Jay, E., 33, 34

Kagan, J., 10, 11
Kahneman, D., 6, 23, 37, 38, 46, 90

Kamenetz, A., 18
Kettler, T., 3
Kohn, A., 18
Krathwohl, D.R., 30, 31
Kuhn, D., 5

Langford, P.E., 28
Lopez, G., 9

Martin, D.S., 33
McClelland, J.L., 32
McCollister, K., 4, 5
McLeod, P., 32
Mlodinow, L., 17, 44
Murphy, P., 4
Murray, B., 33

Nisbett, R., 10, 24, 90
Nitzan, S., 17
Noddings, N., 11
Nowak, M., 41

Ormrod, J.E., 29, 30

Paul, R., 5, 10
Paul, R.W., 11
Perkins, D., 10, 11, 33, 34
Pfaff, D., 41
Piaget, J., 30
Pinker, S., 29, 44, 45
Plunkett, K., 32

Rakow, S., 45
Ramani, G., 4
Ravitch, D., 17
Reeves, A.R., 31
Reynolds, S., 3
Rolls, E.T., 32
Rosenthal, E.C., 10

Rowe, M., 4
Rummelhart, D.E., 32

Sachs, J., 5
Salzberg, D., 17
Sayler, M., 4, 5
Scheffler, I., 33
Siegler, R.S., 30
Sigel, E.E., 30
Silverman, R., 4
Simon, H., 24
Simpson, D., 15, 48
Smolensky, P., 332
Sosa, E., 24, 38
Spataro, S.E., 3
St., B.T., 28
Stanovich, K.E., 34, 38
Sternberg, E.J., 4
Sternberg, R.J., 6, 34, 35, 36, 37

Taleb, N., 24
Taylor, J., 3
Thaler, R., 6, 23
Tishman, S., 33, 34
Tomasello, M., 15
Topping, K., 10, 48, 88
Torff, B., 4
Trickey, S., 10, 88
Tversky, A., 23, 37

Wagner, P.A., 9, 15, 23, 33, 48
Walters, R., 11
Weissberg, R., 3
West, R.F., 38
Wiley, R., 14, 41, 44

Yeh, S., 4

Zhang, Li-fang., 35

Subject Index

Alliance for Excellent Education, 4, 5
American Philosophical Association (APA) Delphi Project, 8, 9
Argue With Me, 88

Bailin, Sharon, 90
Bandura, Albert, 11
Baron, Jonathan, 33–34
Battersby, Mark, 90
Baudet, Stephanie, 88
beliefs, elementary scripts and, 56
Big Ideas for Little Kids, 88
Bloom's taxonomy of cognitive objectives, 30–31
Boole, George, 27, 31
building own scripts, 77–78;
   appropriate language, 82–83;
   critical review, 80–82;
   final considerations, 82–84;
   focus, 79;
   follow up, 80;
   kick off, 79–80;
   length, 83;
   picking a topic, 78–79;
   relevant examples, 83–84
Burroughs, Michael D., 88

California Critical Thinking Dispositions Inventory (CCTDI), 9
California Critical Thinking Skills Test (CCTST), 9

classroom:
   ambience for philosophy, 14;
   conversations, 5–6
Cleghorn, Paul, 88
cognitive emotions, 33
cognitive objectives, Bloom's taxonomy of, 30–31
Coles, Robert, xii
color, elementary scripts and, 57
communities of inquiry, 41–50;
   books on engaging students, 88;
   constructing, 48–50;
   creating, 41–43;
   dispositional values for, 48–49;
   dispositions of individuals and community, 43–45;
   recommended structure, 49–50;
   skills of individual and of community, 45–50
community dispositions, 44–45
community skills, 47–48
concrete operational stage, 29–30
connectionism, 32
contemporary psychological theories:
   Daniel Kahneman system 1 and 2 thinking, 37–38;
   Jonathan Baron and David Perkins, 33–34;
   Keith Stanovich, 38;
   Robert Sternberg and thinking styles, 34–37

critical thinker, 10–11
critical thinking, 17, 18, 19;
    to avoid misunderstandings, 18–19;
    living better with uncertainty and, 21–23;
    programs, 9, 18;
    resources for, 89–91;
    skills, 10
Critical Thinking: Consider the Verdict, 90;z
critical thinking, schools and, 3–5;
    being critical thinker, 10–11;
    classroom conversations, 5–6;
    deliberative thinking, 6;
    reflective thinking, 6;
    thinking critically, 6–10

deliberative thinking, 6–10
Dewey, John, 13, 27
DiMaggio, Joe, 8
dispositions:
    community, 44–45;
    individual, 43–44;
    necessary skills and, 43
dissonance, 7
Durham University, 89

Educating for Intelligent Belief and Unbelief, 20
education, "back-to-basics" trend in, 33
Education Endowment Foundation, 89
elementary scripts, 55. *See also* scripts
epistemology, 17
evil, elementary scripts and, 58
existence, elementary scripts and, 59

Facione, Peter, 90
fast thinking, 46
Festinger, Leon, 7
formal operations stage, 30
Franklin, Ben, 23
fun, elementary scripts and, 60–61

Gestalt school of psychology, 28
Gigerenzer, Gerd, xii, 90
Gilovich, Tom, 90

Gittens, Carol, 90
The Giving Tree, 88
good thinkers, elementary scripts and, 62–63
Great Conversation, 10, 11, 21, 42–43, 47, 48, 79–80;
    definition, 15;
    elements of, 15–16;
    general features of, 42;
    Greek speculations, 16;
    of Humankind, 9, 14, 38, 78;
    institutions support programs to involve students in, 88–89;
    restoring, 17–18;
    scripting path to heart of, 25;
    sitting at crossroad of, 20–21
gut feelings, role of, 24

Halpern, Diane, 7, 33
Harry Stottlemeier's Discovery, 13
Hemberger, Laura, 88
How We Know What Isn't So, 90
human cooperativeness, 41

individual dispositions, 43–44
individual skills, 45–47
Informal Logic journal, 90–91
information processing theory, 31–32
Inquiry: Critical Thinking Across the Disciplines forum, 90
Insight Assessment website, 90
Institute for the Advancement of Philosophy for Children (IAPC), 89
intuition, role of, 24

James, William, 27

kaboom, elementary scripts and, 64
Kahneman, Daniel, 37–38, 90
Khait, Valerie, 88
Kuhn, Deanna, 88

Learning to Think Things Through: A Guide to Critical Thinking Across the Curriculum, 90

legislative thinking style, 35
Lipman, Matthew, 13, 14, 88, 89
Lone, Jana Mohr, 88, 89
long-term memory, 32
luck, elementary scripts and, 65–66

Manoa Uehiro Academy for Philosophy and Education, 88–89
The Mind Club, 29
"Mindware and the Metacurriculum", 10
mindware, of students, xii, 34
Mindware: Tools for Smart Thinking, 90
Montclair State University, 89

Nisbett, Richard, 90
No Child Left Behind (NCLB), xiii
Noddings, Nel, 20
Noise Matters, 78
Nosich, Gerald, 90
Nowak, Martin, 41

Oscanyan, Frederick, 88
Oyler, Joe, 89

Pascal, Blaise, 24
Paul, Richard, 90
Perkins, David 33–34
perspective, elementary scripts and, 67
The Philosophical Child, 88
philosophical inquiry, 18–19
philosophy, xi–xii, 13, 14, 43, 77–78
"Philosophy for Children" (P4C), 13–14, 18, 89
Philosophy in Education, 88
Philosophy in the Classroom, 88
Piaget, Jean, 3–4, 29
Peirce, C.S., 25
Plato, 60, 77
play, elementary scripts and, 68–69
The Power of Critical Thinking, 90
pre-concepts, 28
preoperational stage, 29
principle of familiarity, 84–85
probably/possibly, elementary scripts and, 70

psychological research, thinking theories and;
 Bloom's taxonomy of cognitive objectives, 30–31;
 conclusion, 38–39;
 contemporary psychological theories, 33–38;
 later twentieth-century contributions of psychology, 31–33;
 psychological approaches to thinking, 27–30
psychology, 31–33
Pythagoreans, xi

reasoning, fallacious forms of, 7–8
Reason in the Balance, 90
reflective thinking, 6
The Republic, 77
Risk Savvy: How to Make Good Decisions, 90

Sachs, Jeffery, 4
Sam Houston State University (SHSU) website, 87
SAPERE, 89
schools, critical thinking and, 3–5;
 being critical thinker, 10–11;
 classroom conversations, 5–6;
 deliberative thinking, 6;
 reflective thinking, 6;
 thinking critically, 6–10
scripts, 49–50, 78;
 beliefs, 56;
 building own, 77–78, 85–86;
 color, 57;
 critical review, 80–82;
 elementary, 55;
 evil, 58;
 existence of dinosaurs, 59;
 familiarity principle, 84–85;
 final considerations, 82–84;
 focus, 79;
 follow up, 80;
 fun, 60–61;
 good thinkers, 62–63;
 kaboom, 64;

kick off, 79–80;
luck, 65–66;
perspective, 67;
picking topic for, 78–79;
play, 68–69;
probably/possibly, 70;
sneaking in names of scholars, 84–85;
space, 71;
tips for using, 53;
truth telling, 72;
"why" not as powerful question, 73;
word meanings, 74–75
semantic clarity, importance of, 19–20
Sen, Amartya, xi
sensorimotor stage, 29
sensory memory, 32
Sharp, Ann Margaret, 88
short-term/working memory, 32
Skinner, B.F., 28–29
slow thinking, 46
space, elementary scripts and, 71
Stanovich, Keith, 38, 90
STEM studies, 20–21
Sternberg, Robert, 34–37
structured dialogues, 11
system 1 thinking, 37–38
system 2 thinking, 37–38

Taxonomy of Cognitive Objectives, 35
"Theory of Mental Self-Government", 35, 36t
THINK Critically, 90
thinking:
　children, 29–30;
　critically, 6–10;
　psychological approaches to, 27–30;
　styles, 34–37
Thinking & Reasoning journal, 91
Thinking, Fast and Slow, 90
Thinking Skills and Creativity journal, 91
Thinking Through Philosophy Books 1, 2, 3, and 4, 88
truth:
　search for and wonderment, 16–17;
　telling, elementary scripts and, 72

unavoidable surprises, allowing for, 23–24
University of Hawai'i, 88–89

Vaughn, Lewis, 90
Verbal Behavior, 29
Vygotsky, L.S., 28

Wagner, Paul, 13, 17
Waller, Bruce, 90
Wartenberg, Thomas, 88
Watson, John, 27
What Intelligence Tests Miss: The Psychology of Rational Thought, 90
"why" as not powerful question, elementary scripts and, 73
Wiley, Robin, 78
wonderment, search for truth and, 16–17
word meanings, elementary scripts and, 74–75

About the Authors

Paul A. Wagner, Ph.D., is the author of over 130 publications. He holds a joint appointment in both the College of Education and the College Human Sciences and Humanities at the University of Houston–Clear Lake. He has held various professional affiliations with each of the University of Houston campuses, Harvard, Stanford, Yale, and the University of Missouri. At the college level, he has taught economics, management theory, organizational behavior, development of the sciences, and a variety of courses in philosophy, psychology, and education. He has served on the American Philosophical Association's Committee on pre-college philosophy; he was vice president of the Association of Philosophers in Education and president of its Central Division. He also served as the executive secretary of the Philosophy of Education Society and on the Ethics Committee of the 40,000-member American Association of Public Administrators. He served on the Steering Committee of the Host City Committee of the Second NAFTA Conference and on the board of directors of a number of charities and civic organizations including Leadership Houston. His most recent publications have dealt largely with decision theory.

Daphne D. Johnson, Ph.D., is a professor of education at Sam Houston State University where she received the College of Education Outstanding Teaching Award. She received her doctorate in Educational Psychology and Individual Differences at the University of Houston–University Park. She served as the department chair for the Department of Curriculum and Instruction for seven years bringing project-based learning to the educator preparation program. She worked with Frank Fair and other team members to replicate a study from Scotland on the effects of philosophy for children at a middle school in Texas. For the results, see "Socrates in the schools from

Scotland to Texas: Replicating a study on the effects of a philosophy for children program" (2015a) *Journal of Philosophy in Schools 2(1)*, pp. 18–37, and "Socrates in the schools: Gains at three-year follow-up" (2015b) *Journal of Philosophy in Schools 2(2)*, pp. 5–16. She is on the editorial board of the journal *Inquiry: Critical Thinking Across the Disciplines*. Currently, to further develop critical thinking in students, she directs the website http://thinkingbeyondthetest.weebly.com.

Frank Fair, Ph.D., (University of Georgia) is a professor of philosophy at Sam Houston State University where he received the University's Excellence in Teaching award. He served as the managing editor of the journal *Inquiry: Critical Thinking Across the Disciplines,* and co-authored (with Vic Sower) *Insightful Quality: Beyond Continuous Improvement.* In recent years, his research and writing have been on the theory, practice, and pedagogy of critical thinking, on the creation of communities of inquiry in public school classrooms, and on innovation in organizations. He and Daphne Johnson were members of a team that replicated, at a middle school in Texas, an important study from Scotland on the effects of a Philosophy for Children program.

Daniel Fasko Jr., Ph.D., (Florida State University) is professor of educational psychology at Bowling Green State University. He teaches undergraduate and graduate courses in educational psychology and life-span development, as well as an honors seminar on creativity. He has held leadership positions in the American Educational Research Association and the American Psychological Association, and is a fellow of the Psychonomic Society. He is a frequent presenter, discussant, reviewer, and chair of sessions at national and international conferences. His research interests include critical and creative thinking and moral reasoning. He is former editor of *Inquiry: Critical Thinking Across the Disciplines* and is ad hoc reviewer for *Psychology of Aesthetics, Creativity, and the Arts,* and *Informal Logic.* Fasko co-edited (with Wayne Willis) *Contemporary Philosophical and Psychological Perspectives on Moral Development and Education* (2008) and edited *Critical Thinking and Reasoning: Current Theory, Research, and Practice* (2003). In 2000, Morehead State University honored him as Distinguished Researcher.